THE PERFECT FRUIT

THE PERFECT FRUIT

Good Breeding, Bad Seeds, and the
Hunt for the Elusive Pluot

Chip Brantley

BLOOMSBURY

New York   Berlin   London

Published by Bloomsbury USA, New York

"The Traveler," *The Seven Ages* (New York: Ecco/HarperCollins, 2001),
by Louise Glück, reprinted by permission of the publisher.

All papers used by Bloomsbury USA are natural, recyclable products made
from wood grown in well-managed forests. The manufacturing processes
conform to the environmental regulations of the country of origin.

LIBRARY OF CONGRESS CATALOGING–IN–PUBLICATION DATA HAS BEEN APPLIED FOR.

ISBN-10 1-59691-381-9
ISBN-13 978-1-59691-381-3

First U.S. edition 2009

1   3   5   7   9   10   8   6   4   2

Typeset by Westchester Book Group
Printed in the United States of America by Quebecor World Fairfield

For Elizabeth

CONTENTS

FALLING

1

IT WAS MIDSUMMER then, and I was twenty-seven, and over the course of one month, I fell in love twice. First with Elizabeth: She and I had grown up in the same town, run in the same circles, dated mutual friends. It was only in California, where we both had moved because we were young and it was California, that we really began to know each other and, eventually, to love each other, though we didn't really *fall* in love so much as decide, indirectly but at roughly the same time, to evolve into something more. It was as if someone had flipped the switch on us, rearranged the room in the dark, and then raised the lights to reveal a greater, more spacious arrangement, one in which we sat together to wonder: How did we exist otherwise?

She lived in San Francisco and I was in Los Angeles, so we commuted back and forth on the weekends. I worked as a Web producer for a struggling dot-com near the Sony film lot in Culver City, in a sleek, just-finished office building erected on the site of an old shoe factory. Everything about the company was new—the industry, the business model, the people—so new that it almost seemed not to exist yet. The building's most interesting feature was a massive jumble of steel embedded in its northeast corner. The sculpture resembled a downed helicopter, sinking, and classes from nearby architecture programs came to admire it before the parking lot had been fully paved. Like many of the office buildings going up in that area then, ours looked better than it worked. The building leaked and it sweltered, and the acoustics were warehousian: Sometimes, you could barely make out what your neighbor was saying to you while a hushed conversation from across the giant main room—packed with five-fruit iMacs and hollow-door desks— somehow bounced around the hum of the open floor plan and came in on a wire. You cocooned yourself in headphones; otherwise you were always looking up from your computer, checking over your shoulder to see if the voices were being directed at you. They were rarely directed at me, though. While the programmers programmed and the designers designed, we producers could not be said to have produced much of anything. Instead, as we would later lay out in bullet points on our résumés, we oversaw, we supervised, we managed, and we performed many other vague duties requiring no measurable ability but allowing us plenty of time to reflect on our outside interests. I had a lot of those.

I was fueled by the belief that since there was so much that was possible to like in life, I should try my best to like it all at least a little. After all, if I didn't try something, how could I know for sure that I shouldn't be doing more of it? Among the many pursuits I failed to follow beyond an initial burst of enthusiasm were surfing, reforestation, orienteering, improv theater, home brewing, bass guitar, bullfighting, handicapping thoroughbreds, documentary filmmaking, and political speech-writing. I considered architecture school, film school, and journalism school and went for an interview at an international affairs masters program. Though I joined basketball and softball leagues, I was more often than not a no-show. Every now and then, I attended meetings of the Mars Society. I subscribed to a local theater, at which I caught exactly one Mike Leigh and half a Brecht. I kept an online application for the Peace Corps active for a couple of years but never submitted it. I vowed to get work on an Asia-bound freighter. I went out and drank too often, but had neither a regular haunt nor a favored drink. I was a groomsman in ten weddings, never the best man. I read several novels at once and rarely finished one. Wanting to work with my hands at something, I gleaned scrap metal and old planks of wood, which I kept, unworked, in the trunk of my car. I volunteered to be in charge of selling corporate tables for a charity's annual gala, but then I delivered only one. And it was for lack of trying.

For a while, this skimming of the world's muchness felt meaningful. I convinced myself that I was pursuing the examined life, taking nothing on someone else's word, exhausting my options. But at a certain point, I just felt exhausted. Simple exuberance was not a real embrace of anything and did not constitute a meaningful life. A meaningful life was built of commitments, and that I had none was a cause for brooding. This I liked to do from the top of the unfinished parking deck next to our offices. You could stand on the unrailed edge and look out onto some of the great tropes of the city: the tops of all those palms, the cement-lined Los Angeles River, the Hollywood Hills, and, on some smogless days, the sparkling atoll of downtown. People went up there mostly for the cell coverage—to have a private job interview or a conversation with a girlfriend—but it was also a good place to dwell on all of the nagging questions.

Most days during the workweek, I ate lunch alone at a French-Vietnamese diner on National Boulevard. I sat on a stool at the bar and read for a while from a book or worked the crossword puzzle in a *Times* left on the counter. On Tuesdays during the summer, though, I usually walked over to the Culver City Farmers' Market in the afternoon. They held it on one sidewalk of a small park downtown. The selection was limited, but there was enough to cobble together a lunch, and the market always made for good people-watching: small kids kicking around the grass; their parents and nannies flirting; old people sitting in the chairs in front of the small stage where light jazz and funk bands played; and professionals lingering, on lunch break from the growing number of tech companies and furniture galleries and ad agencies in the area.

A kettle-corn cart anchored one end of the market, and it was neighbored on one side by a coffee trailer and on the other by a bakery that marketed its loaves by giving away thick, buttered slices. In the middle of the market, among vegetable stands, a beekeeper sold honey and a woman displayed home composting kits. At the other end of the park, closest to the community center, fish was sold out of a truck. Between the burrito stand and the Italian-ice man were some tables where you could buy fruit.

I should interrupt this scene and mention here my general distaste for conversion stories. It's not that I don't believe in being *swept away* or *consumed* by something or *seeing the light* or any of those other phrases we use to describe that vital lurch from ignorance to enlightenment. It's more that, in those stories of life's revelatory turning points, the action leading up to the critical moment too often feels contrived, the timing rigged, the light seen retroactively shone. Let it be known then that I am aware that when I tell people about my discovery of the pluot—how it was a warm summer day in southern California, just weeks after I had begun dating the woman I would later marry, but still how I felt empty, distracted, baffled, dispersed, a searcher whose future seemed so unfigured and unaddressed, and how these incompatible feelings were rattling anxiously around inside me and then how, like a winter swim, one piece of fruit cleared all the mess away—it does sound a little like an arc manufactured after the fact to give some transformative drama to an otherwise plain moment.

Because the truth is that the moment was plain enough. I was warm and hungry, and it looked like a plum. It was a soft, dark yellow piece of fruit. When I bit into it, it felt almost liquid, like plum jelly. I ate it outside the fruit tent, bent forward, dripping juice onto the pavement, and I used my two front teeth to scrape off the flesh that clung to the pit. I can't remember what it tasted like really, except that it was so sweet. A moment later, I was right back in front of the woman who had sold me the fruit.

"What is this?" I asked her, and then didn't wait for her answer. "What do you call it?"

I am large and excitable, and I had, at that moment, the fruity rush of sugar in me. She was small and she spoke English only so-so. She shook her head and looked worried. She may have even recoiled. She didn't know what it was called. Part plum though. Maybe it was coming from Bakersfield? Maybe I ask next week? Maybe other know then better?

Next week, I thought. *Next week. Okay. I can wait a week.*

She had other plum-like fruits there, though. She pointed at them. One was purplish and oblong. Another was pink, mottled with green, like something out of Willy Wonka. *How had I not seen these just minutes before?* I thought.

I took five pounds of the fruit back to the office in two plastic grocery bags. Ecstatic about the discovery but slightly panicked about having missed them until then, I called Elizabeth and told her about my find, then spent the rest of the afternoon gunning around the Internet for information on these fruits. But no luck: How do you look for something you can't name?

Later that week, though, at another farmer's market, I found their name. I'd been to this market many times before but had never noticed the sign hanging above four crates of fruit, on which someone had spelled out P-L-U-O-T-S.

I tried to keep it casual, as if the word were not new to me, and, feeling somewhat justified for having majored in French, I asked the man at the stand what the story was with the "plew-ohs."

He looked over at me and said, "PLEW-ott. PLUH-um and ay-prick-OT. Plu-ots."

"Pluots," I said, turning it over in my mouth.

They were, he said, three-quarters plum and one-quarter apricot. Most of them were grown a couple of hours north in the San Joaquin Valley, the vast inland basin of California I had experienced mostly on the fly along its western edge, the long, dry route of I-5 I had driven many times, back and forth between San Francisco and Los Angeles. When I thought about those few times I'd visited the interior of the Valley—a movie set in Bakersfield, a Saturday night bullfight in Madera, a brewpub in Fresno on the way to the Sierras—I could kind of picture citrus groves, but I was fairly sure that I had seen neither plums nor apricots on the trees. As a child of the suburbs from a part of the country thriving in neither fruit, I'm not even sure I knew that plums and apricots grew on trees. That a hybrid of the two fruits could exist was astounding.

There were many varieties of pluot, the guy at the market was saying, each with a microseason. They had names like Flavor King, Flavor Queen, and Flavor Supreme.

"What's the best one?" I asked.

"Flavor King," he said, matter-of-factly. "Hands down."

And that's all it took, really. I don't know if it was the simple thrill of discovery or the joy over what I had with Elizabeth spilling over into other parts of my life, but what my feelings for the pluot felt most like was love. Not, it is probably not necessary to say, romantic love, but surely tied up somehow in the same kind of agitated hunger for more of everything that it stirs in a person. And while with Elizabeth the hunger had evolved gradually but felt sudden and overwhelming, with the pluot it had been sudden and overwhelming but felt gradual. All of my earlier dabbling felt like preparation for this moment. Instead of feeling a sense of *been there/done that*, I felt compelled to know everything about pluots. They were what I'd been waiting for. They were my Thing.

But now that they were my Thing, what would I do with them? Was I going to grow them somewhere? Work in a produce department and sell them? Instead, maybe I would champion them, give them as gifts, walk around town with a big sack of them on my back. Or, maybe I would just eat as many as I could. I did love to eat them. So did Elizabeth. As July faded to August, we found a steady supply of pluots at the markets and the pleasure of them became part of our courtship.

Having found them late in the season, though, we had one more month of pluots and then they were gone. Going solely on precedent, I should have forgotten about them within a few weeks. But I did not forget about them, and six months later I quit my job and moved to San Francisco to be with Elizabeth. And a few months after that, on a warm, drizzly Wednesday in late June, we were both standing in the middle of the middle of California, in an experimental orchard, looking at the creator of the pluot, a man named Floyd Zaiger, who, in his open palm, held a plum.

2

To the northern end of California's San Joaquin Valley, they come every Wednesday in season to look for the perfect fruit. They come from towns down south of Fresno like Dinuba, Exeter, Reedley, and Kingsburg. Sometimes, they come all the way from Bakersfield. Or they come from Oregon or France. Or they come from South Africa, Israel, or Japan. They are fruit growers, fruit packers, fruit shippers, fruit marketers, fruit buyers, fruit sellers, fruit importers, and fruit exporters, and they come on Highway 99, which runs alongside the Union Pacific and creates with that railroad a double spine down the valley. They cut west near downtown Modesto, and just outside of town, they pass a motorcycle dealership, a barbershop, a bodega, a Mexican restaurant, and an ice cream wholesaler. They come through blocks of modest homes, then pass a modest church, a modest canal off the Tuolumne River, and a modest elementary school named in honor of Luther Burbank, the great plant and fruit breeder.

The two-lane road takes an immodest turn after the school, giving way to the new St. Stanislaus church, one of the San

Joaquin's oldest parishes, which recently left its century-old home in downtown Modesto for a massive compound out here in what the wonks call the agricultural buffer zone. Farther along, they pass a local estate of the Gallo wine family and then come on a little farther until they get to Grimes Avenue, an unassuming left turn just before Bob's Taxidermy, which, if passed, is the sign that they've gone too far.

On Grimes, they pass rows of walnut trees and a few ranchettes. The trees they've come to see start then on the west side of the avenue. They give way to a couple of homes, a greenhouse, a trailer. And then they're there, at the small, low-slung house on the right that serves as headquarters for Zaiger Genetics. If they are early enough, they maneuver their truck through the barbed-wire security gate and into the speck of a dirt lot out front. If the lot has already filled, as it usually does well before the nine-o'clock start of these Wednesday tours, or if they are newcomers who are not sure if they should pull all the way in, they park out on the street, under the canopy of a towering deodar cedar.

The first time I went to see the pluots, that's where I parked. Elizabeth was with me and it was her birthday. We'd stayed up too late the night before, celebrating with friends, and having driven out through the fog, we were foggy ourselves. We lumbered out of the car and took deep breaths. The air was muggy from the rain. I stretched, taking in the scene, and a word came to me to describe what I saw: *farm*. It's an easy mistake to make, especially if (like me at that point) you've never set foot on one. It looked, smelled, and felt like what I had always imagined a farm would look, smell, and feel like. The lot was filled with pickups, and a tractor was grumbling in the orchard to the side of the office. Everywhere I looked, I saw what I described in my notes with brilliant precision as "crops." And there was that thick, semisweet smell of dew and soil and fruit. And milling around the front of the house were men with mustaches in boots and hats—and what's not farmlike about men with mustaches in boots and hats?

That's when I realized that we were overdressed. I had on a starched blue button-down and had brought along a light sports coat. Elizabeth was wearing a pink blouse and orange sneakers. We looked out of place, un-farmlike, and having walked into the small, crowded office, we didn't know what to do but stand there smiling awkwardly.

In the year since my initial exposure to pluots, I'd found more information about them, mostly from an article published in 2000 in *Gourmet* magazine by a writer named David Karp (better known in produce circles as the manic, pith-helmet-wearing "Fruit Detective"). From Karp, I had learned that pluots were the creation of Floyd Zaiger, who in his late seventies was considered by many who knew about these things to be the foremost fruit breeder in the world. For his contributions to the realm of fruit, Zaiger had, among other things, been awarded the American Pomological Society's Wilder Medal, the fructicultural equivalent of the Pulitzer Prize. Floyd and his family had started working on plum-apricot hybrids in the 1970s, and almost two decades later they had released their first batch of pluots, among them the Flavor King variety that the guy at the farmer's market had told me was the best. While pluots had started small—in 1994, there were fewer than one hundred acres of them growing in California—the number of trees planted had roughly doubled every year since their introduction. Now there were thousands of acres of pluot trees growing in California (and many more in countries around the world). The audience for the fruit had grown, too. While pluots had begun as specialty items at farmer's markets and in upscale groceries, they were now produce-section staples in large regional chains and Wal-Mart Supercenters.

Perhaps their greatest endorsement had come, in a round-about way, from a list, this too in *Gourmet*, of the best one hundred restaurants in the United States. At the top of that list, *Gourmet* put Berkeley's Chez Panisse, where Alice Waters and company had helped awaken Americans to the pleasures (and pieties) of *mindful* dining. Chez Panisse had been a pioneer in the practice of sourcing the ingredients on its menu, as a reminder (to those who could afford it) that each element of their dinner had been cultivated by or had itself once actually been a living, breathing body. "Rack and loin of Elliott Ranch lamb," "Chino Ranch corn," and "pan-fried Wolfe Farm quail" were not just menu choices. They were branded prayers of thanksgiving. The restaurant was the matriarch of those places, now found in even the most gastronomically barren territory, where the menu changes to accommodate what's in season, what's been just slaughtered, and what's been hauled up from the water. No matter what's on the menu, it's always meant to reflect the Chez Panisse philosophy of taking the best that's locally available, right now—lamb, corn, quail—and elevating, without corrupting, what is essential in it.

That conviction, so prized by the editors at *Gourmet*, was

especially evident in one item the restaurant occasionally served for dessert. In *Chez Panisse Fruit,* Waters wrote that "there is nothing more satisfying at the end of a meal than a perfect piece of fruit." The proof of that came in a simple copper bowl, among the crostata and the profiteroles in the deep of summer: a single Flavor King pluot. It was dark purple, almost blue, and lightly specked with gold. The spicy, sweet flesh tasted of caramel and almonds, and it started dark red just under the skin then bled to a lighter pink near the pit. This piece of fruit had been just picked from the tree at the height of its ripeness, and yet it was uncut, uncooked, undoctored in any way that would seem to justify its role as the finale of a sixty-five-dollar prix fixe menu.

Some naysayers saw it as extreme even for Chez Panisse, evidence that the primacy-of-the-ingredient philosophy had gone too far. The best ingredients should be a given at a top restaurant, they argued, means to an end rather than ends in themselves. Many more, though, saw the pluot as a masterstroke, a brilliant gesture of humility that was the distillation of everything that made Chez Panisse Chez Panisse. What better way was there to illustrate the singular importance of the well-chosen ingredient than by refusing to alter, which is to say refusing to diminish, "the perfect piece of fruit"?

I'd made sure to mention all this when I'd called a week before and spoken to Floyd's daughter Leith. For my girlfriend's birthday, I told Leith, I wanted to take her to the birthplace of pluots. Leith said she'd think about it and get back in touch with me. When she did, a few days later, it was with directions to Zaiger Genetics. She told me that every Wednesday during the season they gave growers and others in the industry a tour of promising new varieties. We were invited. Next Wednesday, eight forty-five A.M. See you then.

We were still smiling awkwardly when a woman—the only one in the room besides Elizabeth—walked over. "Welcome to the birthplace of pluots," she deadpanned. Leith had shoulder-length salt-and-pepper hair and was wearing one of those legionnaire-style sun hats with a drape over the back of the neck. Behind her was an old man standing in the doorway to a small side office. In a soft, raspy voice, he said, "Okay, I think we'll get started."

Leith said, "This is my dad, Floyd Zaiger." He nodded at us, smiling, and said, "Well, I hope you get to see what you came here to see." The brow of one blue eye was cocked higher than the other, and his bifocals were perched at the tip of his nose. He had on a checkered shirt and a tan cap with a logo for the Dave Wilson Nursery on the front. An unattached pair of rainbow suspenders hung over his shoulders like a harness. A canvas satchel was attached to the bottom of each end of the suspenders and in each satchel, he had a logbook. He walked out the door and got in the driver's seat of an old white Lincoln Town Car. Everybody filed out of the office, and Leith motioned for us to get into her white pickup.

The caravan began in front of us, five cars for a dozen or so people, most of them commercial growers who were here looking for new varieties. We slowly pulled behind the office and took a right onto a dirt lane that ran perpendicular to the street. On our left were orchard rows that extended a full block, and on our right was a scattered forest of fruit trees, each one sitting in a blue container tub, like the kind you'd see at a plant nursery.

"What are those?" I asked.

"Those are the female parents for our crosses," Leith said.

I felt a little *uh-oh* plink around my brain. I continued to look out at all these fruit trees and thought *female parents for our crosses*, but the words brought up nothing. So I defaulted to a strategy I would come to rely on over the years I spent talking to Leith about fruit. I asked the same question again but in a slightly different way.

"So what do you do with those?"

"Well, we keep around two thousand trees in containers to use as parents," she said. "Depending on the season, we probably cross eighteen or nineteen hundred in the greenhouse and on all those trees, we'll make anywhere from fifty thousand to seventy-five thousand crosses" on the flowers. To my eyes, the trees all looked pretty much the same—the fruit dangling from scraggly, low branches—but the Zaigers worked not only with plums and apricots, but also with peaches, nectarines, cherries, almonds, apples, pears, and walnuts.

"We tag each tree with a number and label the containers so that we can know for sure what it is." I looked out at the forest of blue containers and saw that each one had a number painted in white across the bottom. I was trying to think of something— anything—to ask, but as we came to an intersection of dirt lanes, the caravan was slowing to a stop. Leith pulled the truck into a row of trees and parked. She reached into the backseat and grabbed some brown paper tote bags.

"You might want to take some samples," she said, handing us a few bags.

We hurried to follow her up the row to join Floyd and the

other men, who were crowding around a tree filled with large, oblong fruit. The fruit was fuzzy and dark with yellowish specks.

"I. S. cot," Floyd said and then rattled off a long sequence of numbers and letters. The other men had paper tote sacks, too. I watched as one of them, a burly man with a big, black mustache, took out a marker and wrote the number on one of his sacks. Like the other men, he circled the tree, looking up at it as if he were inspecting it for something. He plucked off several pieces of fruit, put a few in the sack, and then took a bite of another. Others did the same. Leith pulled off a couple and handed them to us. Unsure of what I was looking for, I took a bite. As my teeth broke through the skin, the juice of the flesh spritzed out onto my sharp blue button-down. But all my attention was on what was happening in my mouth. The fruit was very tart but still sweet, and the texture was fleshy, puncturable. And I was eating it right here in the birthplace of pluots, just paces away from the man many people called the greatest fruit breeder in the world. I looked over at Elizabeth and made a face—big grin, eyes wide, head shaking slightly in disbelief—that was meant to convey something along the lines: "Oh my god! Look what we're doing! Can you fucking believe where we are?" While I was giving her this look, I glanced over to see the burly guy raise his eyebrows, open his mouth, and not-quite-hock what was in it toward the ground. He dropped his piece of fruit and looked back at me. "Oof, that's a spitter," he said, smiling. I smiled back. A spitter? I looked around and saw the others dropping their fruit to the ground. Then, not looking at Elizabeth, I did the same.

Floyd said, "That'll do just fine in France."

Everybody laughed except us.

Meanwhile, Leith had sliced a wedge from a piece of fruit and was squeezing juice onto the glass surface of an instrument that looked like the silver-and-black hilt of a sword. "Twelve," she announced, and some people nodded. "Maybe another week," she said, making a note in a clipboard she was carrying.

"Okay. Well. Onto the next one," Floyd said.

As we walked, I caught up with Leith to ask about the France comment.

"The French tend to like a more acidic piece of fruit. That's what works better over there, where in Asia you generally find that they like the sub-acids, the ones that don't have as much of that tartness."

"So, was that a pluot?"

"No, that was an interspecific apricot—I. S. cot—meaning it's a hybrid of primarily apricot heritage. We're calling those apriums for now."

"So a pluot is three-quarters plum and one-quarter apricot and an aprium is three-quarters apricot and one-quarter plum?"

"Well, that's an oversimplification. In most cases, we've moved beyond a second-generation cross. So you have to look at the genetics of a particular variety. If you cross a plum and apricot, you've got a fifty-fifty hybrid. But then, if you cross that back to a plum, you're three-quarters plum, one-quarter apricot. Then you cross that with another plum, and you're getting different percentages of genes. And we're beyond even that point with most of these. So it just depends on the genetics of a variety. But yes, apriums are heavier in apricot and the pluots are heavier in plum."

I asked Leith about the instrument she was squeezing juice onto. It was called a refractometer, she explained, and it gave a measurement of soluble solids, the concentration of sugars in the liquid. This was called the Brix level of the fruit. The higher the Brix, the more sugar. And for the purposes of these Wednesday morning tours, the more sugar, the better. Twelve was a spitter.

We stopped in front of another I. S. cot. The fruit on the tree was a faded green color, not especially appealing. It was also rock hard and huge, closer in size to a tennis ball than to the more traditional golf-ball size of an apricot. It tasted sweet but also bland, like weak sugar water. More spitting and dropping. Silence.

Floyd: "Why, I thought I'd put a zipper on that and use it as a baseball."

An old-timer wearing a plaid work shirt: "Or Floyd, you could just sell it as a watermelon."

No one kept samples of this one.

I walked alongside Leith and Floyd as we moved on to another tree. They were looking at a long list of codes on Leith's clipboard. The codes represented the dozens of fruits we would be looking at this morning. Each code represented an experimental cultivar and had, in its sequence, all kinds of information, including the tree's location in the 150 acres of experimental test blocks they maintained.

"We call this our COC list," Floyd said. "The Cream of the Crop." He paused and smiled. "We're very scientific."

The Zaigers tried to show as wide a selection of fruit as possible, all the while keeping in mind that what they showed had to be "farmer friendly." The cultivars had to have the necessary qualities to be grown, shipped, and handled like commercial varieties are grown, shipped, and handled, and a flaw in any area would render a fruit useless for serious farmers. A fruit with an exquisite taste that was too small, too dull, or too ugly might not make it as a commercial variety. A fruit could taste like the gods' own creation, but if it cracked before maturity or bruised too easily, then it was an unlikely candidate for commercial growers. Just as important as the taste and appearance of the fruit, said Leith, were the set of the fruit and the strength of the tree. Some cultivars were delicious, beautiful and large, but they didn't produce a high enough yield of fruit on the tree to cover the expenses of growing and picking it.

Still, flavor was more important now than it had been in the past. In the 1970s and 1980s, some growers would decline to taste a variety because they didn't consider the flavor to be that important. Times had changed, though. Reasonable flavor was now a prerequisite. What had made flavor a priority again? Part of it was just due to the cycle of the breeding work being done. For much of the period after the Second World War, breeders were working on size, durability, and color, qualities that would help the fruit make a case for itself in the supermarket era. The older, tastier varieties—the ones about which we like to be wistful—were slowly phased out in favor of larger, harder, and shinier fruit. Once those qualities had been established, breeders began trying to work better flavor back into the fruit. Pluots were just some of the fruits of that labor.

But something had also happened on the growers' end, and it had to do with apples. For years, apple growers in Washington

State and elsewhere favored a big, shiny, highly colored variety called the Red Delicious, which looks good in the store and lasts what seems like forever. One quality the Red Delicious lacks, however, is great flavor, especially when it's picked too early. Because its skin color turns a bright, dark red before the fruit has fully ripened, picking the Red Delicious too early is very easy to do. The Red Delicious became so widespread—by the 1980s, it accounted for three quarters of Washington's apple crop—that it drove down not only the price of the variety but also the fruit's reputation for good flavor. Partly as a result, the Washington apple industry hit bottom in the late 1990s and continued to struggle for years. California stone fruit growers felt that if they didn't watch it, a similar fate would befall their plums, peaches, and nectarines.

So on these Wednesday morning tours, the growers' expectations were high. As we listened to the regulars' rundown of each fruit's flaws, I began to understand how high. One aprium was sweet, but orange and spongy. ("Didn't know you were growing cantaloupes, Floyd.") One pluot was intoxicating, sublime, mottled, and otherworldly, but it was a "stem cracker." Another was so sweet it had sugar rings around the top that looked like the wrinkles of a fruit past its prime. Another suffered from pit burn. Everything we tasted had something wrong with it.

At one point, we stopped in front of cultivar number 142LH560, a plum hybrid that apparently had nectarine in its family tree. (The Zaigers call these nectaplums.) Floyd was looking down at one of his field logs, comparing the fruit in front of him to the notes he'd made about it one year earlier. The other men were circling around the tree, as they'd done all morning, eventually reaching up one by one to pull off a piece of fruit.

"Well," Floyd said, "this one's in its final swell." Leith was slicing into one of the fruits and squeezing the juice onto the refractometer.

Silence for a good ten seconds, and I took the fact that no one had immediately lampooned it as a sign that the fruit must not be a total disaster. Plus, somebody in the group was smiling, a field manager for a midsize grower down in Reedley. He had a half-eaten number 142LH560 in his hand, and he was nodding his head and pursing his lips as if to say, *Not bad*.

"Fifteen," Leith announced, reading the refractometer.

"Fifteen?" He tossed his plum to Leith. "Here, try mine."

Leith wiped clean the glass of the refractometer then squeezed out some juice from what was left of the fruit.

"Now that he's had his sweet lips on it," Floyd said, "it's going to shoot up to twenty-seven."

Leith checked the reading. "Nope. Only twenty-one."

Leith took two more samples from the tree, and both showed Brix levels in the mid-teens. Sweet Lips had picked himself a rogue nectarine.

As we kept on through the Zaigers' orchards, the earlier jokes looped back around. There were more varieties that would do just fine in France. There were more baseballs, more cantaloupes, more watermelons. Floyd began telegraphing his one-liners by smiling wide before talking. At one point, he giggled and then announced that he was starting to "get sugar."

By noon, I was starting to get sugar, too. I felt punchy and flushed, like I'd drunk too much Champagne. It was hot out now and I had tasted an awful lot of fruit. I felt like you do on the second-to-last day of a vacation, when you want to continue in vacation mode, but you've also started thinking about the packing you have to do and the travel ahead of you. And, to be honest, you're kind of ready to get home and get back to the grind you went on vacation to forget about in the first place.

We'd have great souvenirs, though: Even the worst plums of the day had seemed alive and potent in a way that sad-sack grocery store fruit never did, so our threshold for what made a winning variety was so low that we'd put at least one piece of just about everything we'd tasted into our sample tote sacks, which were bulged and sagging under the weight of the fruit we carried. We'd seek out all these fruits again if we could, but it was unlikely that any of the ones we'd tasted would ever make it out of the test block. We'd have them once more as we worked our way through the tote sacks, and then those flavors would be gone forever. We were raising our expectations of what plums could be in a way that we wouldn't be able to satisfy again, and this thought was breaking my sugar-ringed, pit-burned, stem-cracked heart.

The Zaigers always feed their Wednesday visitors, and as we made our way with Leith toward her parents' house for lunch, we passed back by the forest of trees in blue containers.

"So those are the 'female parents for your crosses,'" I said. "When you say crosses, you mean . . . ?"

"I mean, we do what the bees do," Leith said, "except we're doing controlled cross-pollination. We take pollen from trees and we use that to make our crosses, and these"—she pointed at the blue-tubbed trees—"are the trees we pollinate." I was looking at her, trying to concentrate through the sugar buzz. Leith smiled and said, "You know, you'll just have to come back in the spring to see it for yourself."

The next day, I woke and scribbled out my notes from the Wednesday tour. I lined up some of the experimental fruits we'd brought back with us. I stared at them and tried to picture picking each one. I held them in my hand, smelled them. I got a sharp knife and sliced wedges. I ate the wedges and peered in at the insides of the fruits. I took pictures of them, then finished eating them, ruminating. But nothing happened. Before Elizabeth and I had gone to the Zaigers' place, I'd assumed that our trip to the birthplace of pluots would satisfy my curiosity about them. Now, the fruit seemed to hold any number of answers but I couldn't figure out the right questions.

This turned out to be a good thing. While I did want to understand pluots, I wasn't ready for them to be over. So the unsettling feeling of not understanding them was the excuse I had to keep exploring them. Like an old troubadour, I wanted to prolong my desire, not satisfy it. I wanted each answer to make a new question spring forth. Otherwise, what was the point?

My first inkling of that idea came to me in the fifth grade, as I stood in the doorway of the audio-visual room at my elementary school. The school held grades K through six, with kindergarten through second grade on the first floor and third grade through sixth grade on the second floor. Until third grade, you never really had an excuse to go to the second floor, and when you did it was with a discrete task, which you completed with your head down so that when you walked past the open doors of the full classrooms, you wouldn't have to see the older students noticing you walk by. By the end of fifth grade, though, I had traveled both floors thoroughly and had the school mapped out in my mind. I'd even snuck into the cafeteria kitchen during one of the school's open-house nights. The one room I'd never seen was the audio-visual room, which sat at the top of the side stairs, near the cluster of third- and fourth-grade classrooms, and overlooked the school's auditorium. The plain wooden door to the AV room was always locked during school hours, and no light was visible through the crack beneath the door.

The first time I noticed the light on, I was looking up at it from the auditorium stage, dressed in a toga and holding a plastic orange while playing a bit part as a Roman fruit vendor in our school's abbreviated production of *Julius Caesar*. After that night's performance, while we all milled around outside the auditorium with our parents, I hustled up the stairs toward the third- and fourth-grade hallway. At the top, I saw that the door to the audio-visual room was open and I walked in to see that it was a long, tight room that looked down toward the stage, which seemed very, very small. I felt an immediate click of satisfaction, but then that satisfaction was muscled out by a queer sadness at having something end. This was the last unexplored place in the school, and seeing it meant that I could scan through the building now and see how the thing was connected. There were no more undrawn areas in my mental map of the school, and those undrawn areas were what had kept the place interesting. Standing there in the doorway, I felt small, the last unknown place known, my work there done.

And so the goal was to see as much as I could of pluots without hearing that satisfying click in my mind. I wanted to savor them, to string out the knowledge of them. And so that partly explains why, having become obsessed with pluots, which were bred and almost exclusively grown in California, I did the only logical thing and in the spring after our first trip to the Zaigers', left with Elizabeth to live in the apple country of New England.

WINTER

1

WHAT WE IN theory might love about the plum—its fragility, its delicateness, the diversity of varieties available to us—is often what leads us, while shopping, to pass it over for some other, more reliable fruit. Gently pressing the soft, matte skin of a "red" or a "black" plum, we wonder whether this will be a good one or a bad one. We've been burned before. Wistfully, our eyes drift over to the next row, where the clearly labeled assortment of apples gleam hard out from their bins, and the bananas—fruitdom's sure thing—lie uniformly in wait. *Why risk it with a plum?*

This raises a simple truth about plums in the United States: They often suck. Not always. Maybe not even most of the time. But often enough so that it feels risky to buy them. And the problem is not that they're all inherently *bad* plums (though some of them are); it's that they've been picked early, packed hard, shipped for days, stored improperly, and then lumped together into two categories—red and black—which are meant to make them easy to classify but which in the end don't really help us choose a good plum.

Put another way, the problem is not the plums themselves. The problem is what humans do with the plums. Consider, for example, the common red plum/black plum problem. There are so many different varieties grown over the course of the plum season—more than two hundred plum varieties are shipped out of California every summer—and those varieties are available for such a short period of time that it would be impractical to assign each one a price lookup code, or PLU. (A fruit's PLU is the number that goes on those little stickers, the ones that are impossible to peel off a plum without tearing the skin.) To simplify matters, plum PLUs are based mostly on color and size. Four colors—red, black, green, and purple—have two codes each, one for large plums and one for small plums. (There's another code for Italian prune/sugar plums.) This way, supermarket chains can buy plums from many suppliers, move them through their distribution channels and into stores, easily display them in the produce section, and have easily identifiable codes for their cashiers to use to ring up produce at the checkout. Without the PLUs, the logistics of plum-related commerce would be too daunting to manage on the supply side.

For you and me, though, the system makes choosing plums a crapshoot. While the flavor of peaches and nectarines is somewhat homogeneous throughout the season, plum flavors vary week to week. If you really know your varieties—what the skin and flesh colors are, when their maturity dates are, and so on—you might be able to distinguish between the several varieties of "black plums" mixed together in the store at any given time, but even two plums that look alike can have completely different flavors. So the only way to know for sure what a plum tastes like is to take a bite.

As stone fruit people are prone to do, one packer I talked to used apples to draw out the point. "One time, you pick up a Fuji apple and you get Fuji flavor. The next time you pick up a Fuji apple, you get Fuji flavor. Same goes for Granny Smith. Those two apples look different on the outside so you can tell the difference between them. If you want Fuji flavor, pick up Fuji. If you want Granny Smith flavor, pick up Granny Smith.

"Well, you can pick up a black plum with yellow flesh and get the Fuji sensation. And then you can go back a week later and pick up a similar-looking black plum with yellow flesh, and you get a Granny Smith sensation. We often have two different flavor sensations for what looks like the same piece of fruit. People look for consistency when they buy fruit, and we're not giving it to them."

In the supermarkets back east, I was consistently experiencing this inconsistency. And though plums were almost always cheaper than pluots, I sometimes found identical-looking fruit with the same label in both the plum bin and the pluot bin. As often as not, the supermarket's laminated display card had something about how pluots were "three-quarters plum and one-quarter apricot," which I now knew wasn't necessarily true (but was definitely easier for shoppers to grasp). It was also not uncommon to see displays advertising "plucots," "plumots," "plutots," "pluofs," "plutos," "plots" and—my favorite—"plouts," which sounded more like a Bavarian potato dumpling than a hybrid stone fruit. While most stores carried "pluots" (or some close misspelling of them), others had similar-looking fruits that were labeled "Flavor Safari" and "Dinosaur Eggs." Were those pluots, too?

At the end of my first summer in New England, I called Leith to ask her about these labels, and she suggested I get in touch with David Jackson, a fruit grower near Fresno, who might be able to fill me in on the "Flavor Safari" and "Dinosaur Egg" labels. I made an appointment to visit David in December, when there wouldn't be a plum in sight. The last fruit would have been picked during the first weeks of fall, and after a month or two of sorting out the harvest season, collecting the last payments for late-season varieties, and making some basic repairs to equipment, this was when most growers were in the thick of pruning. A week after Thanksgiving, I flew to Los Angeles and rented a car. I was headed back to the Central Valley, American stone fruit's ground zero.

No matter where you're traveling from, to get to California's Central Valley you have to go down. Down in elevation, but also down as in to a lower sort of place, the sort of place you don't want to linger in, like an underground mall parking lot or the stall of a bus station bathroom. The second sort of down does depend on where you're coming from, I guess, but it's at least the prevailing view of most coastal Californians, among whom there's a saying that "California, fifty miles inland, is Arkansas." Anyway, going down in at least the literal sense was what I was doing one hour north of Los Angeles on I-5, just inside the Kern County line, on a six-degree grade in the fog.

Six degrees is the most an interstate can slope and still qualify as an interstate, and you could smell why on the way down. Semis flashing their hazards crept down the far right lane, and the friction from their brakes made the air smell like an underground mall parking lot or the bathroom of a bus still idling at the station. As the December fog broke, I got a first glimpse of the Valley, a little snatch of land to the north that disappeared as the road dipped. Then the view opened again and I could see a whole stretch of the Valley, the curving eight-lane I was on now leveled out below me and jutting into the flat and empty-looking terrain. It was disorienting to look down on the Valley from here; too much altitude and too little distance separated this jagged world from that flat one. The angle just didn't seem possible.

The view reminded me of looking out onto Los Angeles from the Hollywood Hills, where in certain places the depth of field is so compressed, it feels like you could reach down and flip off the lights in all those buildings. The perspective here was like that, except that when I looked out onto the Valley's southernmost point, I could see no buildings, no lights to reach out and flip. Anyway, the scale of Los Angeles is nothing compared to the vastness of the Valley. Surrounded on all sides by mountains except at the inverted delta where what is left of its convoluted river system meets a series of bays around San Francisco, the Central Valley is that enormous trough that occupies the whole middle of California. It stretches nearly four hundred miles long from north to south and up to fifty miles wide. If it were to secede from California, the Central Valley would be larger than ten other states. With a little jigsawing, you could fit Maryland, Delaware, New Jersey, Connecticut, and Washington, D.C., inside its borders. In the relief globe at my local library, the Rockies are shot through with shallow etchings and the Himalayas have vast, open plains draped off of them, but nothing above sea level approaches the complete self-containment of the Central Valley, into which I was able to wedge a piece of macaroni and have it stick.

When people talk about the "Central Valley," they usually mean the more populated, lower two thirds of that piece of macaroni, a region known as the San Joaquin Valley, the southern border of which I was crossing as the interstate carved through a narrow band of foothills and began to flatten out. At Wheeler Ridge, I passed the recently built Tejon Industrial Complex, which houses a nearly two-million-square-foot Ikea distribution center and a Starbucks-Panda Express rest stop. The buildings form the northern outpost of the Tejon Ranch Company, one of the last intact relics of the Mexican land grant era, whose 270,000 contiguous acres make it the state's largest private landowner. The Ikea complex stood almost completely alone at the base of the foothills and the absence of anything around it was unsettling; it felt like bait in a trap. Watching it in my rearview mirror, I cut off the interstate and took State Route 99 north. Off to my left were vast, flat fields where nothing but low scrub grew for miles—how many miles it was hard to say because there was nothing to contrast the nothingness against. It was an empty but developed nothingness, like an endless vacant lot overgrown with weeds from years of neglect. As I drove, other objects eventually materialized. A lone oil derrick, a lean-to, and then, suddenly, an almond orchard. Its plumb rows of leafless trees ran at a sharp angle up to the side of the road, and they brought with them an immediate somethingness to the surroundings. I would learn this about the Valley. Because it's so flat, it's hard to see anything other than what's directly in front of you. And so the impression was usually all of one or the other—nothing or something—and rarely that interplay between the two that passes for a view.

Nearly every written account of the San Joaquin includes a description of its flatness, because that is, apart from its size, the Valley's most notable characteristic. In many places around the San Joaquin, the view still recalls the one Presley saw in *The Octopus*, Frank Norris's classic 1901 novel about the battle between Valley ranchers and the railroad in the mid-nineteenth century: "To the east the reach seemed infinite, flat, cheerless, heat-ridden, unrolling like a gigantic scroll toward the faint shimmer of the distant horizons." Later, the poet Sherley Anne Williams wrote that the Valley was "as flat as a hoecake" (and then added that its summers were "hot enough to fry one"). And in *Assembling California*, John McPhee wrote that the Valley is so flat that it "outplains the Great Plains." Alfred Hitchcock certainly thought so: When he was scouting locations for the classic scene in which Cary Grant is chased by a crop duster in *North By Northwest*, he wanted an absolutely flat cornfield. No location was flat enough for him in the Midwest, so he had corn transplanted from there to the San Joaquin, where he ended up shooting the scene.

Arvin, the first exit off of Highway 99, is a city of less than twenty thousand people at the San Joaquin's southern border.

The only reason you might have heard of it is because it was singled out recently by the Environmental Protection Agency for having the most polluted air in the United States. To be fair, it's not just Arvin (which, passing through, seems pleasant and charming, two metrics the EPA doesn't measure). Other places in the Valley, such as Visalia and Fresno, are also often mentioned when the subject of the nation's worst air quality comes up. And to be fair to the San Joaquin as a whole, it takes the fall for a lot of air pollution that's blown in from the San Francisco Bay area and trapped, with no outlet, in the Valley's box of mountains.

But air quality's not the only problem in the Valley. Six of the San Joaquin's eight counties are California's most poverty-stricken, and the Valley contains thirteen of California's twenty poorest cities. Fewer than half of the Valley's ninth graders graduate from high school, and of those, fewer graduate from college. In the late 1990s, the San Joaquin was labeled a high-intensity drug trafficking area, with as much as 80 percent of the country's meth coming from superlabs operated across the Valley, which also has—by a long shot—the state's highest per capita rate of violent felonies and property crimes. In fact, four cities in the San Joaquin—Stockton, Visalia, Modesto, and Fresno—recently landed on a top-ten list tracking American cities with the highest annual number of cars stolen per one hundred thousand people. The list wasn't all bad news for Modesto, though, which fell to number five on that list after several years as the car theft capital of the United States. (Unfortunately, that didn't stop the editors of the 2007 edition of the *Cities Ranked and Rated* guide from listing Modesto as the worst city in America, period, a title for which it barely nudged out two of its neighbors in the Valley, Merced and Visalia.)

With the nation's worst air pollution, the San Joaquin has an asthma rate that is much higher than the state and national averages. Chronic health problems such as asthma and obesity, for which the Valley has the highest rate in the state, are less likely to be regularly addressed in the San Joaquin, where a quarter of the population has no health insurance. But even for those who are healthy and well-insured, it can be hard to breathe in the Valley, where during the summer it's not uncommon to see ten straight days of temperatures above 100 degrees Fahrenheit. Those heat waves result in deaths and power outages and all-around disgruntledness, which, in extreme temperatures, the governor has tried to remedy by opening emergency cooling centers at fairgrounds, where the public can go and sit together under state-sponsored air-conditioning to ride out the misery and wonder why the hell anybody ever settled here in the first place.

Originally, it was wheat that brought all the settlers. Since wheat didn't have to be irrigated, it was a perfect crop to plant in the naturally dry interior. As a result, it ruled inland California in the second half of the nineteenth century, absorbing much of the labor force that had flooded the state during the Gold Rush. The Valley floor was so totally covered in wheat that, as Kevin Starr, California's state librarian from 1994 to 2004, recorded, "a plowing section might work all day to reach the end of one field, camp there overnight, then plow its way back all the next day, repeating this process for days on end until the work was complete." Meanwhile, the tracks of the Southern

Pacific railroad were opening up markets in the East and making more lucrative specialty crops—such as stone fruit—a possibility for growers in the San Joaquin. Tie-by-tie, on its way from Stockton southward, the railroad opened up the middle of California. When no town existed where a town was needed, the railroad would do what it had done all across the West: stake out a town grid, with the numbered streets parallel to the tracks, the lettered ones perpendicular.

By the mid-1890s, as wheat peaked in a glut, settlers had begun to hack away at early irrigation projects to make use of the groundwater and the rivers of snowmelt that ran down the slopes of the Sierras and spilled onto the Valley floor. As they began to control, divert, and irrigate, and were able to plant thirstier, generally more demanding crops, those early farmers discovered that the Valley floor contained a remarkably rich mixed bag of soil types. By the time the first Valley wells were pickaxed in the 1800s, the Sierran snowmelt had been replenishing the aquifers for thousands of years so that the San Joaquin sat atop one of the most abundant stores of groundwater in the world. The control of that groundwater and the snowmelt from the Sierras—the water's "reclamation"—is what has made the San Joaquin possible as a fertile, habitable place. The homegrown irrigation of the late 1800s grew into municipal-controlled water districts, which led to state aqueducts, federal reservoirs, agencies, and water alliances. For most of the twentieth century, the U.S. Department of the Interior's Bureau of Reclamation joined forces with the state to control every river that flowed into the San Joaquin and to reengineer those rivers for maximum efficiency (or according to the prevailing political will). The modern map of the San Joaquin's waterways—both the natural and artificial ones—looks like the blue scribblings of a toddler who's just learned to operate a crayon.

That reengineering of the waterscape, coupled with the great expanse of flat, fertile earth and a climate that is as Mediterranean as anything in the United States gets—with cool winter nights and dry, hot summers—made the San Joaquin an ideal inland outpost for what librarian Kevin Starr called California's emerging "fruit culture." The Valley absorbed settlers from all over—post-Confederate Anglo-Saxons, Okies, Swedes, Portuguese, Basques, Armenians, Lebanese, Japanese. In and around the railroad towns up and down the Valley, all they had to do was ready the land, steer the water, and grow the fruit, and that's what they did—as Starr noted in his book *Inventing the Dream*, "the 30 tons [of fruit] of 1869 becoming the 70 tons of 1870, the 1,571 tons of 1880 becoming the 81,976 carloads of 1906." By the end of the First World War, California—with the San Joaquin as its heart—produced more of just about every fruit and vegetable than every other state combined, a dominance that still holds today.

And yet this fruitfulness was not obvious driving through Bakersfield, one of the fastest-growing cities in modern America. Here, on this late Sunday afternoon, abutting the highway just past the "Welcome to Bakersfield" sign, was all the indication you needed of where the Valley was headed: On the east side, an enormous cement wall blocked the highway's view into an unfinished housing development; on the west side, the same thing, except a great red balloon hovered above one of the wall's corners as an invitation to visit (and an unintended advisory). Off the highway, more housing compounds: Cantabria, Lavender Trails, Casa Bella, Mayfaire. Then the predictable Starbucks and Loew's, and a building so recently conceived that its only identification was "Future Outlet." From 2000 to 2005, the population in the Valley grew by almost 17 percent, much faster than that of California as a whole. And though things had slowed down recently, as foreclosure rates skyrocketed across the Valley, the state still estimates that the San Joaquin will grow by at least one million people every decade until 2050, which means, barring some hard-to-imagine reversal in patterns, more overburdened schools, more pollution, more asthma, more car thefts, more car thieves, and more reports like this one from the Visalia *Times-Delta*: "Work crews were still cleaning up Thursday after a five-car train derailed and sent two boxcars full of mozzarella cheese tumbling to their sides six miles northeast of Visalia." And more morning TV news traffic reports like this one: "We've got a traffic advisory of the fruity kind! A big rig that was hauling peaches slammed into the guard rail, and unfortunately, Ryan, there are peaches scattered all over [Route] Ninety-nine. We have a lane closed, and peaches are clear over in the number one lane."

For years, Valley agriculture has had a reputation more for its quantity than its quality. This, the San Joaquin, is one of the places where people point when they want to talk about what's wrong with what we eat. While the Midwest handles the corn, this is where the single-crop megafarms pump out the raw ingredients for our industrial food system. With the three highest-producing agricultural counties in the world, this is where Big Ag supplies Big Food. Here's how big: Tulare County does one billion dollars in milk every year. Kern County's annual pistachio crop is worth $275 million, which is nothing when compared to its $315 million in carrots and its $450 million in citrus. And from Fresno County, which is home to more than three million turkeys but only one million humans, growers ship $600 million in grapes, $500 million in almonds, $475 million in both tomatoes and poultry, and at least $100 million of a dozen or so other crops, including plums.

On the spectrum of economic and cultural value, the California plum falls somewhere in the neighborhood of insignificant. A fickle, minor crop, the plum is more valuable than relative newcomers to the state, such as the persimmon or the pomegranate, but it's nothing to more established resident fruits, such as the peach, the grape, and the orange. Still, nine out of every ten plums grown in this country, and practically every pluot, are grown in the San Joaquin, and most of these come from a nook between Visalia and Fresno, with the greatest concentration along the watershed of the Kings River, from the town of Reedley near the Sierran foothills down to the highway towns of Traver and Kingsburg. That's where I was driving after sundown, on the lookout for a place to stay.

2

DAVID JACKSON'S EXTENDED family radiates across Kingsburg, a town situated right at the border of Fresno and Tulare counties. Kingsburg is so densely populated with Jacksons that some people simply call the town "Jacksonville." Sun-Maid's headquarters are here and historically the area around Kingsburg has been a table grape and raisin area. But the oversupply of those crops over the years led to heavy stone fruit plantings as well.

The night before, I'd found a motel in Selma, a town bordering Kingsburg to the north. At various moments in *its* history, Selma has been called the "Home of the Peach" and the "Raisin Capital of the World." Today, though, it's best known for its smorgasbord of shopping centers and chain stores lined up along the highway.

Still on eastern time, I woke early and went out to stretch my legs. In the parking lot, I could barely make out the cars through the low, dense fog, and as I walked through the neighborhood around the motel, the street lights were dim blots above me. Back in my room, I flipped on the local morning news and heard the weather man report that area schools were on a "foggy day" schedule—all buses delayed or canceled. I'd heard about the Valley's legendary "tule fog." Named for a type of sedge that once grew all over the wetlands of the Central Valley, the tule fog is a high-inversion fog, a bottoms-up weather event that usually starts after a rain when the wet earth cools the air just above ground level. That air condenses, and because the Valley is boxed in by mountains, the lower store of cool air is pushed down by warmer air on top and has nowhere to go. So it just sits there, like a bored ghost. Several days of near-zero visibility can pass before the fog disperses, and the longest recorded tule fog lasted thirteen days at the beginning of 1954. In 1963, the week after President John F. Kennedy was shot, parts of the Valley were covered for nine days with a gloomy tule fog that never rose above one thousand feet.

The fog is brutal on humans—even a day or two of it can make a person long for the sweltering sun of August—but since it keeps the temperatures in the low- to mid-forties day and night, the tule fog is great for fruit trees, which go dormant in the winter. During dormancy (which is the tree version of hibernation), the trees recover from the long summer and regroup so that their buds can develop normally and grow well in the season ahead. Dormancy is measured in chill hours, one chill hour being one hour below 48 degrees Fahrenheit. Each fruit variety needs a different number of chill hours over the course of the winter and without enough of them, the trees will emerge from their dormancy erratic, like a bear stirred too soon from its cave: The buds might be weak and more susceptible to damage, or the flowers might bloom too slowly or not enough. So what you hope for if you're a grower (or breeder) of stone fruit is that from December all the way through the end of January, the temperature stays below 60 degrees Fahrenheit in the daytime and below 45 degrees Fahrenheit at night. The tule fog helps make that happen.

By late morning, the fog had risen off the ground and was hanging low in the sky in a solid, gray plate. I drove down to Kingsburg for breakfast and ate a plate of Swedish pancakes at a place right off Highway 99, which runs at an angle along the west side of town. Many of Kingsburg's earliest settlers were Swedish, and driving around town on my first full day in the Valley, I could see that heritage on display everywhere—a restaurant called the Dala Horse, flags of the Scandinavian cross hanging from street lamps, a windmill at the Shell station. Kingsburg's Main Street looks like Main Streets all over the San Joaquin, except here all the businesses bid you *Välkommen*, even the Mexican restaurant.

I met David Jackson at Denny's. I was surprised when I saw him. On the phone, his voice had been soft, almost gentle; but he turned out to be a striking, built bear of a man, like a hybrid of Cary Grant and Lou Ferrigno. He reminded me of a couple of football coaches I'd had, not just because his forearms were the size of my calves, but also because he had a thing for aphorisms.

I'd mentioned my trip to the Zaigers' and my curiosity about what drove a grower to look for new varieties. "Variety selection is the most important thing we do as farmers," David said, pointing a spoon at me for emphasis. "If you've got a variety that's not producing or that too many other guys are growing,

then you've got to find something else. You can't will that variety to be a success. It's like the old saying 'If your horse is dead,
dismount.' "

The patriarch of the Jackson family was David's father, Hershel Jackson. Hershel and his wife, Clara, were born in north-
eastern Tennessee, where they were married in 1933. They
moved to California a couple of years later. They had one daughter and three sons—David's the youngest—and they both lived
into their mid-nineties. By the time they died a couple of years
ago (only ten weeks apart), they had eighty-seven descendants
spread out over five generations. The Y chromosome is strong
in the family's line; as one grower put it, "Jacksons like to have
sons." All but a handful of the Jacksons live within a dozen
miles of the original home ranch in Kingsburg. To a one, the
working adults are in agriculture. Together, they control somewhere around fifteen thousand acres of fruit in California. Half
of those fifteen thousand acres are controlled by a sales company called Kingsburg Orchards, which is run by David's older
brother George and his sons. Most of the company's acreage
lies within a massive compound southwest of town, just off the
Kings River. For the past twenty years, Kingsburg Orchards has
flourished by focusing on "specialty" items, including avocados,
Asian pears, kiwis, and persimmons. But it's mostly known as a
stone fruit operation, and some of its riskier investments have
been into what are typically thought of as high-end novelties—
things like black apricots and saucer peaches. Still, if you were
playing a word association game with someone in the California fruit business and you said, "Kingsburg Orchards," the first
thing that would come to most people's minds is the word

"pluot." Kingsburg Orchards started planting Zaiger varieties in the 1980s and the Jacksons were some of the first growers to invest heavily in pluots.

David was an independent grower then who used Kingsburg Orchards to pack and sell his fruit. But after a while he began to feel like just another Jackson. So he finally struck out on his own and started a company called Family Tree Farms. With his sons and his son-in-law, each of whom had his own farm, he bought a packing facility east of Kingsburg in a town called Dinuba. The previous occupant was a company called Apio, which specializes in packaging fresh-cut vegetables. Apio had bought the shed from Cargill, the multinational corporation that had managed to become the world's largest supplier of grain but—like many other big companies, including Dole and Del Monte—had been waylaid by fresh stone fruit, which was too fickle, too unpredictable, too hard to mechanize. "Cargill lost millions trying to get into stone fruit," David said. "Plenty of the big guys have tried to get into stone fruit but they've failed because they don't understand it. My dad's always had a saying: 'Nothing grows well unless your shadow's on the soil.' If you're not out there getting your boots dirty—checking maturity, deciding when to pick, figuring out how many people you need to do it—then the wheels start falling off. Bad things start to happen. Cargill and all the other large companies who have come out have failed, because they don't have their shadow on the soil." He paused and then said, "You know, plums aren't like carrots."

A lot of people in California stone fruit had carrots on the brain, because the biggest commercial packing shed, Fruit Patch, had recently sold a chunk of the company to a private equity firm that had brought in a CEO from the carrot industry. Commercial packing sheds are ones that pack and sell fruit for a bunch of different growers, none of whom is large enough to support its own packing house and sales team. Fruit Patch packed and sold fruit for dozens of different growers, and the new Fruit Patch CEO got off to a bad start when he reportedly said that he was "going to do for stone fruit what he [had done] for carrots," meaning he was going to work the inefficiencies out of the system. The coming season would be his first in stone fruit, and everyone was watching Fruit Patch to see what would happen. The general feeling was something along the lines of David's assessment: Plums aren't like carrots, and one man's inefficiency is another man's shadow on the soil.

If David's shadow was the one *on* the soil at Family Tree, Kingsburg Orchards' shadow was what hung *over* the place. When David had first started Family Tree, it had been tough to distinguish himself, but he and his sons and his son-in-law now had close to four thousand acres of stone fruit. That was only half of what Kingsburg Orchards farmed, but still it was no small amount of land to keep your shadow on. Like Kingsburg Orchards, David's Family Tree Farms grew a lot of pluots and hybrid plums. In fact, the two companies grew a lot of the same fruit and had a similar philosophy about how to sell and market it. In an industry in which durability, color, and size were the main selling points, the Jacksons' collective war cry was "Flavor!"

"Here's why I started chasing flavor," David said, glancing over his shoulder at the booths behind him. "My strongest competitor in the field"—he rarely mentioned Kingsburg Orchards by name—"got an exclusive deal on a black apricot. I started hearing in the woods that if the buyers wanted these black apricots then they were going to have to start buying some other stuff from this competitor, too." It was flavor and novelty as leverage. "So—you know, I know these guys real well—I went over to them and said, 'Hey, I want some of that black apricot.' They said, 'Are you kidding me, man?' So I had a decision to make. I could stay in the boxing ring and get pounded, or I could start fighting. I decided to start fighting."

Over the course of a couple of years, David traveled to the major commercial stone fruit growing areas of the world—Chile, southern Europe, Israel, South Africa, Australia, New Zealand—and he met breeders and sampled fruit. He cut his own exclusive deals on all kinds of stuff—ginger-scented apricots, 28 Brix plums—and when he returned from his walkabout, he was as clear-eyed as he'd ever been. He'd seen the future and it was flavor. No more ho-hum varieties for him. If it didn't "eat well," then Family Tree Farms wasn't going to grow it. While most of the fruit trees were still in federal quarantine, mandatory for all imports, David would get the first round of them out to plant in the coming year.

"I went back to this competitor and I said, 'Hey, I just want to thank you for not giving me that black apricot. You could have had me right there, but instead you made me five times stronger!'" He erupted in a high-pitched peel of a laugh, loud and fast, that filled the room. But then he turned suddenly serious. "But that competition makes us all stronger. Dad always said, 'It takes two people to make a champion.' When I wrestled, he said to find the best guy in the room to work out with.

Well, I love the competition, but I just want to win. I want to have that flavor bar up to where they have to beat me. So I'm raising the bar to eighteen Brix." Failure, to paraphrase Truman Capote, was the condiment that now flavored his success.

Unlike Fruit Patch and other commercial sheds, Kingsburg Orchards and Family Tree are vertically integrated companies: The only fruit they pack and sell is their own. According to David, this makes it easier for them to project how much fruit they'll have in any given season, when it will be coming off, and what the overall quality will be. "If I'm packing sixty different guys' fruit, then that's sixty different attitudes I'm dealing with," David said, still pointing the spoon. "So you're trying to take sixty different attitudes and put them all in one box. That consistency, that quality is going to vary. And you're only as good as your last box."

That mantra was true for everybody, but it was especially important for Family Tree and Kingsburg Orchards, who were always shouting "flavor" from the rooftops. If flavor was your competitive advantage, then that's what you had to deliver. Because a variety lasted just a couple of weeks, it was hard to promote and build a market for just one variety of fruit. To help combat this fast turnaround, both Jackson outposts had created premium labels to brand the plums and pluots they sold. Each of their labels would be applied to upward of a dozen varieties during the course of the season, each one cycled in at the moment of its peak ripeness.

The main Kingsburg Orchards label was for a line of mottled red plums and pluots. The brand was called Dinosaur Egg, and the PLU sticker that went on the fruit featured a cheerful apatosaurus (think Fred Flintstone's work crane). Going head to head with Dinosaur Egg was Family Tree's label, Flavor Safari, which had seven mascots—a coterie of wild animals, including a rhino, a giraffe, and a gorilla.

While the two lines included many of the same varieties, both companies were aggressively working to replace some of their existing varieties with high-Brix plums over which they had exclusive control. If truly consistent flavor was impossible over the course of a season, then the Jacksons wanted to obviate the need for consistency by growing fruit that had so much flavor that nobody cared if this week's plums tasted different than last week's plums. Using a dinosaur and the animals of the African savanna, they hoped to get the fruit buyer to go by brand, yet imagine he was going by flavor.

3

MY LIFE HAD begun to feel like that old Tootsie Roll commercial: Whatever it was I thought I saw became a pluot to me. I saw them everywhere I looked, and even if something didn't have anything to do with pluots, I still found a way to relate it to them. This, I think, is a common symptom of love. Almost every book I read during this period has pluot-related notes scribbled on the insides of its cover, and I kept a running file on my computer where I recorded my pluot version of Deep Thoughts:

"Plums in Iraq?"

"Pluots: Are they an absorption or a diversification?"

There were even some signs that I was dreaming about pluots: One winter morning, I woke up and found that in the night I had scribbled the following message on a pad I kept by the bed: *e pluribus unum prunus*. Out of many, one plum.

When I came across a poem by Louise Glück called "The Traveler," I printed the first part and hung it above my desk. It seemed like a sign:

At the top of the tree was what I wanted.
Fortunately, I had read books:
I knew I was being tested.
I knew nothing would work—

not to climb that high, not to force
the fruit down. One of three results must follow:
the fruit isn't what you imagined,
or it is but fails to satiate.
Or it is damaged in falling
and as a shattered thing torments you forever.

Still, I began to find that loads of people had heard about pluots, and they didn't always see the fruit in the same way I did. Articles about the Zaigers popped up in newspapers and magazines, and in many of them, the Zaigers were made out to be mad scientists of the white-lab-coat-and-crazy-hair variety. For example, in a *Wired* magazine breakdown of modern fruits in which two Zaiger hybrids were mentioned, the introduction read: "We love Twinkies, Slim Jims, and any kind of processed cheese-like spread. Let's face it, those food scientists toiling in the basements of transnational conglomerates know what's tasty. Not to be outdone, produce growers are taking a shot at engineering superfoods . . ." And on *ABC's World News with Charles Gibson*, the reporter intoned: "If you've paid attention to what you buy at the grocery store, you may have noticed that *fruit has changed*. Where once there were dependable McIntosh apples, red plums, and yellow peaches, now the fruit displays are arranged with such exotics as the Gala apple, Pinto peach, Pluot, and Nectaplum . . . A peach is no longer just a peach. Much of the fruit today . . . is designed or *outright invented.*" Naturally, this iffiness about what pluots were and how they were developed spilled over and was magnified on the Internet, where I regularly read blog posts condemning the pluot as just another genetically modified Frankenfood that corporations were trying to push down the throats of an unsuspecting public.

This wasn't what I imagined the fruit to be, and fortunately I had read books—about fruit and breeding—and so understood that pluots weren't genetically engineered in the lab. Like the "dependable" old McIntosh and yellow peach, pluots were the result of selective breeding of the sort that had been around practically since the dawn of agriculture. They weren't altered using any system more sophisticated than the ones that bees had used for as long as bees had been around. In this sense, they were genetically engineered in the way that pretty much every fruit in the produce section—and the farmer's market—was genetically engineered.

The closely related stone fruits—almonds, apricots, cherries, nectarines, peaches, and plums—belong to a genus called *Prunus.* Recent research points to one common ancestor for all the stone fruits—a bitter almond—but today, botanists recognize hundreds of different *Prunus* species.

While the world's roster of plums is vast and varied, just about every commercially grown fresh plum in California is a descendant of *Prunus salicina.* The varieties of that species are known as "Japanese plums" because Japan is where their recent ancestors were imported from starting in the late nineteenth century. In fact, older records of these plums have been found farther west, in China, where *Prunus salicina* has been eaten fresh for thousands of years and has been known by thousands of names. (The Taoist sage Laozi observed that "the names that can be named are not unvarying names," and while he wasn't—as far as I know—referring specifically to plums, he did have the good fortune to be born under a flowering plum blossom tree, whose five-petaled clusters are sacred in China.) Many of the varieties that thrived in the wild in China were cultivated and improved for centuries by the Japanese, who were no strangers to plums; pits found there date back more than two thousand years. Plums were sold in the markets of Edo seven centuries ago, and later, during the feudal wars in Japan, the roving samurai would subsist in part on *umeboshi*, sour plums that had been pickled and dried and could last for years.

In central and eastern Europe, archaeologists digging around in prehistoric ruins have found pits from plums that resemble *Prunus domestica*. Today, that species is the most common of the so-called European plums, a general name which, as with the Japanese plums, has more to do with where they were popularized than where they came from in the first place. Were these plums taken to Europe from the Caucasus, from ancient Assyria? Maybe. Alexander the Great probably carried some of these varieties back from western Asia after his conquest of much of it in the fourth century B.C. Some historians do point to Alexander's Greece, but many more point to classical Rome as the place where European plums were first domesticated on a large scale. In volume twenty-three of his thirty-seven-volume *Historia Naturalis*, Pliny the Elder mentioned Rome's "great crowd of plums"—this was in the first century A.D.—and then he went on in some detail to describe the medicinal effects that juice steeped with dried plums could have on the bowels. Taking the point of view that many have adopted before and since then, Pliny thought that *Prunus armeniaca*, the apricot, was just another type of plum.

Over the years, as plums were carried along trade and war routes, they were resettled and renamed. In the Middle Ages, more varieties of *Prunus domestica*, as well as varieties of *Prunus insititia*—the damson plum—found their way back to Europe in the packs of the returning Crusaders. Most damsons are sour to the point of inedibility, but their high acid content made them ideal for jams and preserves. Plums may have arrived in England much earlier, as *domestica* pits have been found in Iron Age digs, and stones resembling damson pits have been found in excavations of Roman camps there. Then again, those pits could be from bullaces, blue and tart like damsons, which grew wild in England and had been cultivated at least by the fourteenth century, in time for Chaucer to write about them in the gardens of monasteries there.

By the sixteenth century, England was full of plums. In mid-July 1545, one of Henry VIII's warship's, the *Mary Rose*, set sail to do battle with the French. While preparing to engage, the ship unexpectedly heeled over and was lost. Though survivors' accounts differ—only a handful made it out, while five hundred or more souls sank with the ship—one popular scenario has it that the *Mary Rose*'s gun portals had been left open after a round of fire, and water rose above them and overtook the ship. However she was lost, the ship was a favorite of Henry VIII, and the crew had been fed accordingly. Having rediscovered the *Mary*

Rose in 1966, excavators later found barrels of cattle carcasses, pig bones, venison, mutton, and preserved North Sea cod; peppermills; and a large basket of plum pits, five varieties in all. Researchers believe that the fruit had been fresh, picked just before the *Mary Rose* had gone to sea.

Across the channel, France was cultivating its own share of plums. The Agen plums of the southwest—which centuries later would be the foundation for the California prune market— had enough sugar that they were still sweet when dried. The Mirabelles, yellow and honeyed, were eaten fresh and were used to make brandy. Another one, a yellowish green plum called the Reine Claude, probably originated in present-day Armenia. Like a lot of fruit, it trickled over the years westward into Italy and then drifted up to France. There, it was named for Claude, the wife of François I (who watched with his navy as the *Mary Rose* sank). The fruit is syrupy-sweet, round, and small enough for most people to fit whole into their mouths. Later, a Paris-based English minister named John Gage sent the plum to his brother, Sir Thomas Gage, in Suffolk. The tag identifying the fruit was lost along the way and so Sir Thomas's gardener, stuck for a name, just called the plum the "Greengage." (Other sources suggest that the plum was the namesake of a Sir William Gage who brought the plum from France himself. Still others claim that the fruit had been circulating around England under the name Verdoch since the early 1600s and that some Gage or another was merely the first person to distribute it widely.)

By the late seventeenth century, botanists were beginning to uncover the mechanics of plant life. In the 1670s, Nehemiah Grew gave a presentation to the Royal Society, in

London, putting forth the idea that plants had a sex life. Several years later, he published *The Anatomy of Plants*, in which he wrote that a plant's stamens were its male parts and that the pollen in them carried reproductive cells and was therefore the plant's sperm. A decade and a half later, at the end of the seventeenth century, the German botanist Camerarius discovered that the stamen and pistil were both necessary for a plant to reproduce, though it wouldn't be until later that scientists figured out exactly what did what inside the flower.

By then, Europeans had been exploring the New World for two hundred years. Having come across the Mississippi River in 1541, the Spaniard Hernando de Soto found along its banks several types of wild plum. These were varieties of *Prunus americana*, the most widespread of the twelve plum species native to North America, which grew in a patchwork from New England to the Gulf of Mexico, all the way west across the frontier. The first colonists brought their own seeds and plants from Europe, but soon after landing, the Pilgrims encountered beach plums, *Prunus maritima*, the small, wild fruit that grows along the eastern seaboard of the United States. In 1621, after the Pilgrims' brutal first winter in Plymouth, Edward Winslow wrote of the discoveries: "Plums of three sorts, white, black, and red, being almost as good as a Damson." Ten years later, plums were growing alongside "smalnuts, hurtleberries, and hawes of whitethorne" at the "Governor's Garden" of John Winthrop, the first leader of the Massachusetts Bay Colony.

As more Europeans settled in America, native and imported plums spread out from Massachusetts across the colonies. The Dutch planted them in New Amsterdam, and later, in Virginia,

George Washington had plums growing at Mount Vernon, some of which he had grafted from the then-famous orchards of Colonel George Mason. Like Washington, Thomas Jefferson favored greengages. In North Carolina, John Lawson, the surveyor general of that territory, described the first efforts on the part of European settlers to domesticate a native species. He called it the "American Damson" because it resembled the plum he knew so well from the Old World: "We have the common, red and black, which bear well. I never saw any grafted in this country, the common excepted, which was grafted on an indian plum stock, and bore well . . . Their Fruit is red, and very palatable to the sick. They are of a quick Growth, and will bear from the Stone in five years, on their Stock." This "American Damson" turned out to be a variety of beach plum, which is one of the most stubborn plums to domesticate. Considering this, Lawson got spectacular results with the plums. Typically, his success with fruit didn't translate to larger temporal rewards; years later he was taken captive by locals and tortured to death with splinters of burning pine.

In 1737, the great Swedish taxonomist Linnaeus published *Hortus Cliffortianus*, a breakdown of the famous gardens of the Dutch banker George Clifford. In it, he first used the word *Prunus* to describe the genus of stone fruits. Linnaeus split *Prunus* into four subgenera: *prunus* (plums and apricots), *amygdala* (almonds and peaches), *cerasus* (cherries), and *padus* (bird cherries). Later, he grouped them all into just *prunus* and *amygdala*, but the Swiss botanist Augustin Pyramus de Candolle redivided them into five subgenera. Since then, the various cherries have been split into several subgenera, and peaches have earned their own subgenus *persica*, so named because they were believed at one time to have originated in ancient Persia. (Now it's thought that peaches made it to Persia on trade routes from China.) Many contemporary pomologists, convinced that all the stone fruits have one common ancestor, no longer bother with any of the subgenera and instead break *Prunus* out just according to species.

The same year Linnaeus published his *Hortus*, the Prince Nursery of Long Island was founded by Robert Prince in New York. It was the first commercial nursery of any note in the colonies. In 1771, the Princes became the first nurserymen to publish a catalogue of their varieties. It listed thirty-three plums, among them the greengage, the Yellow Egg ("as big as an hen's egg"), the White *bonum magnum*, the Drab d'Or, the Carline, the Early Sweet Damson, and the Fotheringham. (Fifty years later, the nursery would claim to have nearly one hundred fifty plum varieties.) The note at the bottom of the one-sheet catalogue left explicit directions for the interested fruit grower:

> Any person having a mind for any of the above trees, and choose to have them sent to New-York, they can have them sent on Tuesday and Friday of every week, as there is a boat that constantly goes from Flushing to New-York on them days, and may commonly be found at Burling's Slip (John Yates, master). If any person should want to send their orders for trees, and the boat should not be there, they are desired to leave them with Mr. William Field, merchant, at the head of Burling's Slip, in New-York.

Various Princes authored important plant-related treatises, which were, following the Revolutionary War, important tools for spreading the word about the theories and mechanics of horticulture. (Before independence, there were no established means by which farmers could share information with each other. But in the new republic, Americans created agricultural societies and farming organizations to report their findings on issues such as fertilization, pest control, and pruning—issues that had, until then, been mostly neglected.)

In 1790, William Prince oversaw the first significant experiment in American fruit breeding, when he planted twenty-five quarts of pits taken from an orchard of open-pollinated greengage plums. (Open pollination is done by birds, bees, wind, or some other natural force that leaves the pollen source unclear.) Of the thousands of pits that he planted, Prince selected only a handful of productive offspring, though four of these lasted for many years. He called them the White Gage, the Red Gage, Prince's Gage, and Washington, the last in honor of the first president of the new republic.

By the early nineteenth century, plums had rumbled out onto the American frontier. Wild plums had been there all along, but as settlers went west, they began to cultivate native and European plums. In 1814, a man named William Dodd, who had served under Andrew Jackson in the Tennessee militia, planted plum pits at a farm near Knoxville. The pits Dodd planted had come from either a local Creek chief or the banks of the nearby Tallapoosa River. Either way, they were a variety of *Prunus hortulana*, another native plum species. One of the offspring bore fruit and was propagated, initially, under the name Old Hickory (and then, also, General Jackson). In 1824, Dodd and his brother relocated to Illinois, taking some Old Hickory budwood with them. Dodd settled in Springfield, where the variety became known as William Dodd and Chickasaw Chief. His brother moved north to Galena, where his plum was called the Hinckley. Meanwhile, the same plum had somehow ended up in Pennsylvania, where a man named Miner got his hands on it and disseminated it in large enough numbers that it came to be known as the Miner plum and was recognized as the first distinct variety of domesticated native plum. It was prized mostly for its hardiness in climates too cold for other common varieties. In a lukewarm endorsement of the plum, the editors of one journal in Wisconsin wrote that "it must be quite obvious that the Miner plum cannot even be considered second rate in quality. Still, on the principle that half a loaf is better than no bread at all, it may be safely recommended to those who have neither the time nor the opportunity to grow finer fruit."

4

Julius Milton took no fruit with him when he set out for California after the American Civil War. Having enlisted in the Confederate States Army at the age of sixteen, Julius had served as courier for Brigadier General Rufus Barringer of North Carolina. At the war's end, with the South in tatters, Julius sailed by way of the Isthmus of Panama. He landed in San Francisco and began ranching near Stockton. By the 1890s, he had saved enough money to buy forty acres from the railroad in the town of Parlier, in southern Fresno County, just west of the Kings River. He ran sheep over the thousands of uninhabited acres between his ranch and the Sierran foothills. He started off growing mostly alfalfa, but by 1900, he'd also planted some grape vines and stone fruit, probably an old peach variety like the Muir, something that he could dry. From there, he moved to canning peaches like the Orange Cling and the Palora. The entry on Julius in the *Historical and Biographical Record of the San Joaquin Valley*, published in 1905, noted that in addition to "carrying stock in the Grower's Winery at Parlier," Julius was "interested in all movements pertaining to the general community in which he [made] his home."

You could say the same about Rod Milton, one of Julius's great grandsons. The California Tree Fruit Agreement is the growers' organization for peaches, plums, and nectarines in the state, and Rod has, at one time or another, volunteered to serve as the organization's chairman, as its vice-chairman, and as a member of its Executive Committee, Peach Commodity Committee, Nectarine Administrative Committee, California Plum Marketing Board, Research Subcommittee, Tree Fruit Quality Subcommittee, and several other ad hoc committees and task forces. (He's also a regular churchgoer and hunting safety instructor.) On the CTFA Web site, Rod's "Meet the Grower" page says: "According to Rod, he wants each variety to create an experience that ranks with a first kiss, a grandma's smile, the last day of school, and outside fastballs over the right field fence."

Rod is lean and tidy. He wears large glasses and a dark mustache and, more often than not, a full-brimmed hat. By the time he came on the scene in the 1950s, the family was growing fruit for the fresh market. It was common then for someone to have forty acres covered with just a few varieties—maybe some Thompson grapes, some Santa Rosa plums, and some Sun Crest peaches. The Miltons were more diversified than most; they had a rough dozen varieties of stone fruit and some Thompsons. They started picking on June 1 and were often finished by the third week in July.

Like many family operations then, the Miltons did their own

packing. At six every morning, the men on the family's small crew started picking into large buckets. When a bucket was filled, it was carried to a mobile packing rig that had a corrugated roof on it for shade. The rig had three packing stalls on each side with gravity-controlled conveyors. Rod's mom was the head of the three-woman packing crew. She packed six different sizes of plums; to determine the fruit size, she had a series of steel rings she could hold in her hand for comparison. It was a ten-hour day, and when you got finished with it, you knew that you had worked.

"You still had some Okies in those days, people who'd come out from the Dust Bowl," Rod said one afternoon when I visited him. We were sitting in the Miltons' airy living room, in stocking feet, surrounded by books. "I remember the Prince family, Jack and Luella Prince. Jack seemed like he was twelve feet tall. He could outpick everybody. He picked with two buckets instead of one and probably picked twice as much as everyone else. And he picked only for Luella. Nobody would argue with that, because she could outpack everyone. My dad would watch her and say, 'Now, there's a professional.' She would sit there packing with a cigarette dangling in her mouth. The ashes would get longer and longer and longer, and you would watch it and watch it, and you'd think that the ash was surely going to fall, but then at the last minute she would flick it. It was amazing."

When Rod was a child, the Miltons grew the kinds of stone fruit we now like to lament no longer having. Blazing Gold and 49er peaches. Early Babcocks. Dixon clings. Early Elbertas. Nubiana plums. Casselman plums. "That was a *superb* plum. All those old plums just had incredible flavor—El Dorado, Laroda,

Burmosa, Santa Rosa. But man, with something like the Santa Rosa, there's no forgiveness with the pick date. You absolutely have to be ready. It can ripen overnight. You know, you go out and look at it one afternoon and think you're three days away, and then the next morning you look at them and you say, 'Oh my god! I've got to get all these off right now!' Santa Rosa is a lot like an apricot that way. It's brutal. It can be ready to pick at eight A.M. and then be dead by noon."

That finickiness goes a long way in explaining why California growers were beginning in Rod's early years in the business to move away from the old classic plums. They were too small, too dull, too fragile. As supermarkets grew and distribution channels became sophisticated enough to spread California's stone fruit all over the country, the stores' buyers wanted fruit that was bigger, redder, harder. So out went the Santa Rosas and in came the Angelenos, the Blackambers and Friars—workhorse plums that were forgiving on the pick. If you don't get to Friars on Tuesday, you can wait until Thursday. You may lose something in flavor, though. Friars, Milton says, "are not bad plums. But they're not Santa Rosas either."

In part because of its general farmer friendliness, Rod still grew Friars, even though there were newer varieties that tasted better. One patch of his Friars he helped his dad plant in 1965; they were the oldest trees Rod had in his orchard, and though he was ready to pull them out and replace them, he was keeping them around as long as he could afford to. "For my dad," he said. "For nostalgic reasons."

Nostalgia is a common condition among stone fruit growers in the San Joaquin. Rod's stories reminded me of the stories my dad has told me over the years about the summers he hitch-hiked out west to work on a combine, harvesting wheat, oats, and barley. The crew would start the season down in Burkbur-nett, Texas, and then work its way through south-central Okla-homa, western Kansas, and finally into eastern Colorado. So that the combines would keep running, the crew ate lunch one at a time, and if it was your day to go last on the lunch shift, the thought of the spread waiting for you would start to break your will by about noon. One of the summer's last jobs was cutting Moravian barley on Coors land; the field manager would bring you out a cold can of beer at the end of each day, and you sat there in the fields, drinking, watching the big, red sun dip be-hind the Rockies.

I also thought of my friend Harrison, who grew up on a ranch east of Marysville in the 1930s, and who, when I told him about all the new housing developments going up in the San Joaquin, recited from memory part of the preface from J. M. Synge's 1907 play *The Playboy of the Western World*:

In a good play every speech should be as fully flavoured as a nut or apple, and such speeches cannot be written by anyone who works among people who have shut their lips on poetry. In Ireland, for a few years more, we have a popular imagination that is fiery and magnificent, and ten-der; so that those of us who wish to write start with a chance that is not given to writers in places where the springtime of the local life has been forgotten, and the harvest is a memory only, and the straw has been turned into bricks.

My favorite of Harrison's stories was the one he told about the title match between Joe Louis and James "The Cinderella Man" Braddock in June 1937. Harrison listened to the match on the radio in the main ranch house, which had only recently been wired for electricity. When the ranch hands returned from the round-up later that night, Harrison stood on the porch of the bunk house and recited the call of the fight, word for operatic word, until Braddock was beaten down enough and the referee stopped the fight in the eighth.

Never mind that those aren't my memories; there's no room for your real past in nostalgia, and given the choice between, on the one hand, a twelve-foot-tall Jack Prince carrying his two buckets of plums to Luella, who was always almost but not quite dropping ashes onto the ripe Santa Rosas she was eyeballing for size and, on the other hand, trucks dropping off pallets at the bay of a spotless commercial packing shed where Friars were being sorted by infrared optical sizers and then guided down a chute for a woman in a hairnet to pack, I wanted Luella and Jack, the buckets, the cigarette ashes, the Santa Rosas, the metal rings you could hold in your hand. Who wouldn't? (On one trip to the Valley, I was sitting in the office of another grower who was probably born around the time Rod was planting those Friars. His family's business had started small but had grown over the years into a massive farming operation. By all accounts, he was a wealthy man, still relatively young, with a family, top of his game. We were talking about the modernization of the stone fruit industry and as he described it, he became increasingly frustrated by what he was hearing himself say. Finally he stood and walked over to a metal filing cabinet.

"You know what? I'll tell you what I want. I want to have fun again." He handed me a framed photograph. In the picture, he and his brother were children. They were working on a modest packing line. Their parents were there in the picture, too. Everybody was smiling. "That's what I want. *That* was fun.")

Not that Rod was living in the past. He couldn't afford to. He had a reputation as a sober realist when it came to growing stone fruit, someone who had successfully navigated the transition from growing fruit as a way of life to growing fruit as a business. His 103-acre orchard, which was a blend of the sturdy and the sublime, reflected this. His goal was to have around twenty-seven varieties spread out over the season, sometimes more but rarely fewer than twenty-five. Two-thirds of the varieties he grew were plums and pluots, and while he did grow some workhorses like Friar, he also had some lesser-known varieties, such as the Grand Rosa plum. As a small grower, he had very little room for flops but he also couldn't afford to ignore potential hits just because they were a bigger risk. Though he rarely made it up to Modesto anymore for the Wednesday fruit tours, he always had an eye on the new fruit that was coming out and he was willing to gamble on unproven, newer varieties that he loved. He was one of the first growers to test an early Zaiger hybrid called Flavorosa, and he had lots of newer Zaiger varieties as well. Having little room to plant a proper test orchard, though, Rod resorted to grafting several varieties onto single trees. For this reason, he liked to say that he was growing "two hundred trees of one scaffold." It wasn't for the novelty: Rod believed that the new pluot varieties were quickly changing the marketplace for plums. Growers could now reasonably expect to offer a plum that was large, firm, and highly colored enough to please a chain store's fruit buyer but that had some of the great flavor that had disappeared with El Dorado, Casselman, and those memorable plums of an earlier generation. While plenty of growers had gone out of business for taking too many risks, many more had been ruined by being too complacent and ignoring the reemergence of flavor.

Rod did confess that there was one variety he grew at a total loss. When he saw it for the first time, he knew that there were problems with it. But when he tasted it, he said to himself, "I've got to have it. I've just got to have it." Rod had thirty trees of the variety and though he never packed and sold it, he just couldn't bring himself to pull it out—it was *that* good. Against his better judgment, Rod kept convincing himself that somewhere someone—an ice-cream company, a jam maker, one of those fruit strip outfits—would finally figure out what to do with a fruit as divine as Flavor King.

5

ON THOSE MORNINGS when I woke up in the San Joaquin, it was my habit to lie in the motel bed, listen to the trucks on the highway, and wonder how the air outside would smell. Some mornings, it was synthetic and sweet, like bubble-gum-scented air freshener. Some mornings, it was skunky and loose. Other mornings, the Valley's feedlots lent an animalic undertone to the air. Even though the ocean was hours away, it wasn't uncommon to be hit by one of countless marine smells, an entire spectrum of which could wash over the Valley: the fishy underside of a wharf, the floating puddle of harbor scum, the bucket full of bad oysters. There were mornings that reeked of diesel fuel and others that reeked of citrus. Once in a while, both came at me equally and the result was a smoky Cashmeran, like a sweaty pub full of pipe and ale. Occasionally, I was blessed with a light breeze that blew across almond blossoms and left a delicate, floral sillage in its wake. More often, the Valley just smelled like shit.

The morning after I met Rod Milton, the air had an apple-cider-like quality to it. The fog had burned off to reveal the snowcaps of the Sierras, and a deep purple sky set the backdrop for a fleet of battleship clouds above. I drove a dozen or so miles east to Reedley, a town near the Sierran foothills that has traditionally been the heart of the Valley's stone fruit belt. Most of the growers, packers, shippers, salesmen, and marketers who make up the California stone fruit industry live within one hour of Reedley. This proximity to each other has a tendency to make fruit people tight-lipped about the industry. Often, I'd introduce myself to a grower and, after chatting for a few minutes, he'd say, "Well, listen. I'm happy to give you my impressions, but I wouldn't ever want my name used." Or, "If you want to run some ideas by me, I'd be happy to tell you if you're on the right track." Or, more to the point, "We like to keep to ourselves." Sometimes, I felt like I was in Los Alamos. When I brought up this closeness-to-the-vest quality with one big packer, he said, "Imagine if all the big tire companies were right next to each other so that the people at Goodyear went to church with the people from Michelin. We are all each others' neighbors, but we're also each others' main competitors." The result seemed to be that everybody knew something about everybody, but nobody knew everything about anyone else.

I had tracked down John Kaprielian, the burly mustachioed guy Elizabeth and I had met at Zaiger Genetics on her birthday. Since we'd met John, his family's fruit business, Kaprielian Brothers, had been sold to the Ballantine Produce Company, one of the industry's oldest and largest commercial grower-packer-shippers. Ballantine had started in the 1940s as a commercial packing house. Over the years, the company had backed into farming, and now it packed and sold its own fruit as well as fruit from other growers, all of which went out as Ballantine product. As with Fruit Patch, one of the main challenges Ballantine faced was trying to make sure that growers were tending to their trees in the right way and picking the fruit at the right time and size so that each box of fruit Ballantine packed was as much like the last one as possible. As a member of Ballantine's grower services department, this was part of Kaprielian's job.

For most of its history, Ballantine was known as a plum house, but now it shipped pluots, yellow and white peaches and nectarines, apricots, grapes, and a handful of other things. In the early 1990s, when Wal-Mart opened its supercenters and began selling produce, Ballantine started shipping the retailer a little stone fruit. It had since become one of the store's leading suppliers of plums and nectarines. During the off-season winter months, it supplied North American stores with stone fruit and grapes from Chile. Today, though, there was little activity at Ballantine's main packing shed, a large, low facility in the middle of a giant, fenced-in paved lot just outside of Reedley.

I met Kaprielian in a trailer next to the main building. He was with Rick Milton, Ballantine's head of grower services and—small world—Rod Milton's brother. They were preparing for a meeting with all their field managers, whose job this time of year was to listen to and counsel Ballantine growers on the coming season. Though there was no fruit on the tree, everything the growers did during this time of the year was important—when and how they thinned their trees, what and where they sprayed, which of their varieties they kept or pulled out.

"The challenge is to get all the fruit from these different

growers locked into a system that it can't get out of," said Milton, as we sat down around a conference table. "You have to work with the growers on cultural practices—thinning, pruning—and then on maturity, and you have to be very, very strict on sorting so that you put out a consistent product."

When I asked how the recently completed 2006 season had gone, Kaprielian said that while it hadn't been a particularly good year for fruit quality, it had gone okay in terms of sales. That was one of the odd things about the fruit business, he said. Some years, the conditions were just not right to grow great-tasting fruit, which required the cooperation of many things—most notably the sun—that were simply out of the growers' control. But when the conditions weren't ideal, it usually meant that there was less fruit available to be packed and sold. When there was less fruit being packed and sold, it meant that those who were packing and selling fruit were making money. Fruit quality was no match for supply and demand.

On the other hand, said Kaprielian, there were some years when the conditions were perfect and the fruit was as good as it could be, but you still lost a lot of money.

"Like 2004," Milton said. "That year, there was blood in the streets."

"What happened in 2004?" I asked.

"Too much fruit, too few buyers," Milton said, matter-of-factly. "We all had a good box of fruit, so all we had to differentiate ourselves was price." He explained that the box price was usually high right at the beginning of the season, when stores wanted to get the first of the summer fruit and weren't so concerned with what it cost. The number of orders and the box price at the start of the season—usually the middle of May—set the tone for the next couple of months. In 2004, retail buyers saw that there was a lot of fruit to choose from and negotiated better box prices. Then, said Milton, "we all kept dropping the price on each other. It was a bloodbath. After that, we saw some consolidation on our end and we saw a lot of people get out of the business altogether."

"So when people sat down and thought about whether—"

"Nobody had time to *think* about anything! The banks did the thinking for them," Milton said. "And we've lost fifteen percent of our total volume over the last few years." The downward trend in the industry had been apparent for years, they said, but 2004 was when everything came into clear focus. They pointed out a chart on the wall that showed the volume of peaches, plums, and nectarines over time. (Because so many people who grow plums also grow peaches and nectarines, and vice versa, and because those three fruits have the same trade organization, they're often lumped together. You'll often hear people talk of the "total packout" for "PPN"—peaches, plums, nectarines.) The total number of boxes of PPN shipped had gone from almost sixty million in 2003 to just over fifty million in 2006. The most precipitous drop of the chart was in plums, already the least grown of the three fruits. Plums were in a free fall, their volume having dropped 20 percent since 2003.

A lot of growers were pulling out stone fruit and moving to crops that were easier to harvest, store, and ship: walnuts, almonds, olives. Others were getting out of agriculture completely and selling the development rights to their land (making way for the new houses and strip malls that hopscotched up and down the Valley—scattered orchards giving way to bulldozed corner lots with "Coming Soon" signs oriented diagonally so that comers from all directions could read the name of the future neighborhoods: Sun Villas, Orchard Pointe, Olive Lane, Rustic Oaks).

But these changes on the grower end weren't the real causes of the drop in volume. They were the effects of two major changes that had been under way for years on the retail end. The first change had to do with how retailers thought about fruit as part of their pricing strategy.

"Just picture a brick wall with a hole in the center and on one side of the wall, there's us with all this fruit," Milton said. "And on the other side of the wall, there's the retailer out in the produce section of the store. Well, it used to be that no matter how much fruit we shoveled through that hole, the retailer would keep up with us. If we were shoveling real fast, then he'd be on the other side of that wall grabbing fruit and putting it out in the store real fast. You could call the buyer and say, 'Look, I've got all this fruit and we'll give you a dollar off each box, but we really need to move it.' And he'd say, 'Okay, send it.'"

While almost all of the products in a supermarket—crackers, mouthwash, canned soup—remain consistent and static from store to store, fresh produce is one of the few ways a store can distinguish itself from its competitors. This is why it's almost always the first thing you see when you walk into the grocery store. Traditionally, fresh produce has been a loss leader, a hook that supermarkets knowingly lose money on to lure in customers. During strawberry season, for example, a store might stock up on strawberries and run an advertised two-for-one special, on the theory that people will come for the discounted strawberries and then stay to buy everything else at regular prices. This has been the supermarket way pretty much since the dawn of supermarkets, and traditionally produce buyers were receptive to letting the supply of fruit partially dictate what they ran on special. This time-honored strategy could be seen in the annual "plum-o-rama." If California plum growers had more plums than they knew what to do with—as is the case by August in most years—then they shoveled the fruit through Milton's brick wall, with produce buyers standing there on the other side taking all those plums—black ones, red ones, green ones, yellow ones, purple ones—and stacking them up in a prominent pyramidal heap just inside the store's entryway.

But over the years, the Wal-Mart way of "everyday low prices" for consumer packaged goods had also been rubbing off on produce departments. More and more, supermarkets wanted the produce section to pull its own weight. If every other section of the store was analyzed according to how much it netted the company per square foot, then the produce section would be analyzed in that way, too. Produce buyers started moving away from the inefficiency of having to react to the fluctuations in supply, and they started ordering according to what the spreadsheet told them. "Screw Mother Nature: Here's how many plums we need and here's when we need them." The days of the plum-o-rama were fading.

"So now it doesn't matter how fast we're shoveling fruit," Milton said. "The retailer's worked out how much fruit he can take and that's how much fruit he's going to take, period. The supply can speed up but he's staying at the same pace. So we've got all this fruit stacked up against our side of the brick wall." Seen in that light, the 20-percent drop in plum volume from over the previous few years was not so much a decline as a correction. It probably wouldn't be the last one, either, said Milton. "We've got a ways to go. The volume we have now, while it's dropped considerably over the past few years, still seems to be too high."

The second major change was the consolidation of supermarket chains, which were constantly under pressure from box stores and discount clubs.

"How does the consolidation affect stone fruit?" I asked.

The Ballantine field managers were starting to trickle in for the meeting. "You know, you should really talk to David Albertson, the owner of Ballantine," Kaprielian said. "His family's been in produce a long time, and he could tell you about consolidation. He's always saying, 'Why can't the stone fruit business be like OPEC? Why can't we just tell them what they'll pay?'"

Later, I did catch up with David Albertson. We made plans to get dinner at a restaurant in Fresno that serves Armenian-Cajun cuisine. (Fresno has a big Armenian population and, apparently, a few Cajuns, too.) Albertson is something of an anomaly in California stone fruit. He was born in Boston and attended Harvard, where he played hockey well enough to continue after graduation as a semipro defenseman for the Phoenix Apaches. His family, who was in the produce business up north, got into citrus down in Florida and then took a stake in Ballantine in

1950. Eventually, they bought out the other partners. Albertson has lived all over the world tending to family business. He got into the juice concentrate business and, for a while, held a seat on the New York Cotton Exchange. He lives most of the year in Winter Park, Florida, where his wife, Judith, is an art consultant and dealer. When he goes to the Valley on Ballantine business, he stays in an apartment at a hotel near the restaurant. When I went to pick him up there, the hotel bar was filled with people attending a National Onion Association conference. A wide, genial man in his seventies, Albertson was wearing black suit pants and a light blue, open-collared dress shirt.

At dinner I asked him about the idea of an OPEC for stone fruit—being able to control the volume and price of the fruit being sold to retail buyers. He smiled a grim smile and leaned back in the booth. First of all, he said, an OPEC of any kind was not possible in the United States; cartels and price fixing are illegal. Secondly, even if it were legal, collusion among the sales teams of the big packing houses would be next to impossible because none of them really trusted each other. The only sensible reaction to retail consolidation was an equal and opposite reaction on the industry end. It, too, had to consolidate.

"Our industry is totally dysfunctional. It's a classic case of reverse leverage."

I shook my head. I didn't get it. His BlackBerry was buzzing on the table—*bzzzt bzzzt*—but he ignored it and started explaining. "When Ballantine went into business in the nineteen fifties," he said, "Sanger had fifteen packing houses and Reedley had ten. That was twenty-five in just that area around there." There were packing houses all across the southeastern San Joaquin then, some of them big and commercial, some of them little more than a sturdy table set up in the orchard. Over time, though, packing houses started consolidating to cut costs and to handle a larger volume of fruit. By the end of the 1970s, there were still dozens of smaller packing houses, but the industry was essentially controlled by a group of commercial packer-shippers called the Big Eight. Ballantine was one of them.

Most of the sales filtered through the Big Eight, and with hundreds of retail buyers and brokers on the other side of that brick wall, there were plenty of people who were willing to take however much fruit the industry shoveled through. And there was plenty to shovel. As commercial packers, the Big Eight contracted with individual growers for the course of the season. A packer took a commission on each box packed and sold for its growers, so the system tended to reward volume. The more boxes you shipped, the higher your commission. It was a seller's market, and the industry could afford to think in terms of volume.

But by the mid-1980s, consolidation on the retail end was under way, and stores were just beginning to rethink the flow coming through that brick wall. How much fruit a store carried began to be dictated by the finance guys and not the produce guys, and the formula for stocking the produce section began to reflect that. Instead of reacting to supply—"California's got a lot of plums right now, so let's do an ad and run them on sale"—the retailers began to think, "How much do we need in this space to make such and such an amount?" Instead of *more* fruit, many buyers started asking for *bigger* fruit, and growers who wanted more control over how they navigated this shift in the business began to break away from the Big Eight and do their own sales.

"Eventually, in the nineteen eighties and nineties," David said, "you had—and I'm just making this number up—two hundred packing houses and two hundred sales companies, while over this same time, the opposite was happening on the buyer side, where you began to see consolidation across the board." His Black-Berry went *bzzzt bzzzt*, but he didn't look at it. He ordered tea and short ribs.

It was starting to make sense. If, on the one hand, you had eight major packing houses responsible for selling most of the stone fruit grown in the United States, and, on the other hand, you had dozens, if not hundreds, of fruit buyers in regional grocery chains, produce distributors, and independent brokers, then you had a situation in which the fruit growers had the advantage. But when you went from that setting to a setting in which you had hundreds of packing houses and sales companies and only a relatively few centralized buyers—Kroger buying Ralph's and Whole Foods buying Wild Oats and so on and so on—then the buyers had the advantage. Reverse leverage.

Buyers weren't just using their leverage to influence volume and price. They were also dictating how the fruit was packaged. For years, stone fruit was almost always volume-filled in rectangular boxes: twenty-eight pounds of peaches or nectarines per box and twenty-five pounds of plums. The number of individual pieces in a box depended on the size of the fruit. But once retailers got the upper hand in the relationship, they started asking for all kinds of different pack styles: clamshells, Euro

Boxes, Panta Packs, IFCOs, club pack bagged. Eager to close the deal, most sales companies and packers said yes, and they said yes so often that buyers began to assume that they could get the fruit packed in any style they could dream up—in sealed tennis ball cans if that's what they wanted.

"But everybody talks about this as if it's the retailer's fault, and it's not, because we're the ones making the sales," Albertson said. Stores like Kroger's were getting scrunched at every end by Wal-Mart and the club stores. And the only places it could make up the difference were in produce, meat, dairy, and flowers. "They have to turn the screws on the suppliers of those things, so that means that the people who supply fruit are negatively affected. On top of that, we've done a horrible job of managing the commodity." *Bzzzt bzzzt.* "We're completely inefficient. Some of these inefficiencies are just the cost of doing business—a plum is not a cash commodity like a soybean." Or, David didn't say, a carrot. "But some of these problems are due to fat in the supply chain. Too many carnivores out there. Too many marketers. Too many salesmen."

Whatever the causes for this reversal in fortune, the bottom line could be seen in three related graphs: If you looked at a graph of the average wholesale price for a box of fruit from the 1970s until today, it would show a sawtooth pattern, up and down depending on the year. But if you looked at a graph of the industry's costs—labor, fuel, equipment—it would go up and to the right, a steady increase over time. And if you looked at a graph showing the average retail price of fruit—what we pay at the store—it too would go up and to the right, a steady increase over time.

"*That* is the story," David said. "Box price stagnant. Costs rising. Retail price of fruit rising." It was an environment that favored economies of scale. For the small- and medium-size growers, the writing on the wall was clear and bleak.

Still, there was always hope for the new season. Spring was coming, and what happened in spring usually set the tone for the summer to come.

SPRING

1

I TOOK LEITH up on her offer and flew back out in the
spring—in February, actually, which in California felt like
spring. February is the most important month for a breeder of
stone fruit in California because it's when most of the breeding
happens. If the dormant trees have had plenty of winter chill
hours, they tend to bloom out uniformly (and usually produce a
stronger set of fruit later in the spring). Occasionally, if you've
had a cold early winter, and you get mild temperatures starting
in early February, everything may seem to bloom at once. This
"flash bloom" doesn't happen too often. But in January, a freeze
had hit certain areas of the San Joaquin Valley. The freeze had
destroyed a lot of citrus and avocados, but because peaches,
plums, pluots, and nectarines had still been in dormancy, the
cold had merely ensured that they slept a deep, hard sleep. By
February, California's stone fruit had had more than a thousand
chill hours and emerged with a strong, uniform bloom. When I
showed up, the air was warm and sweet, and just about all the
crossing was finished. After several sun-up-to-sun-down seven-
day workweeks, the Zaigers were all exhausted and slap-happy.

Their trees were starting to blossom, which was pretty, but there wasn't a whole lot for them to show me out in the orchards.

Still, Leith met me one afternoon to give me a quick lesson in fruit breeding. We hopped on a golf cart and her dog Sadie climbed to sit astride us. Rain had just come through, and the orchards were muddy and quiet.

On paper, the techniques used to breed stone fruit seemed pretty straightforward. The fruit we eat is the end result of pollination, the sexual fertilization of a plant. Peaches and nectarines are mostly self-compatible, which means they can fertilize themselves with their own pollen. So to cross peaches and nectarines, you have to emasculate their blossoms first. This way, they're not able to pollinate themselves before you're able to cross them with whichever pollen it is you want to cross them with. To emasculate a blossom, you have to strip it of everything but the pistil, the female sexual organs of the flower. You can do this in several ways. Pinching a blossom with your fingers is the simplest way, if not the easiest. You have to squeeze the blossom hard enough to get all the male parts but not so hard that you pull off the female parts, too. Some people find it less dicey to use tweezers.

Plums, however, are almost entirely self-incompatible. That means that they cannot pollenize themselves and so need the pollen of another variety to set fruit. (This is why you never plant just one plum tree in your backyard.) This fact of life sours many growers on plums, because they have to worry not just about the variety of plum they want to grow and sell, but also about the pollinator for that variety. But for a stone fruit breeder, plums are a little less of a hassle during the crossing season because you don't have to emasculate them. You still have to worry about bees getting to the plum trees with some other pollen, but to prevent that you can cover the trees with netting or, as some breeders do, build small houses around the trees.

Let's say you have a variety of plum called Victoria Sykes and you want to pollenize it with a variety called Jack Horner. Ideally, you're able to time the cross in such a way that when the blossoms of Victoria Sykes are just opening to reveal the pistil inside, the blossoms of Jack Horner have not yet opened into flower but are about to. This is called the "popcorn stage," because that's what the blossoms look like. You pick the popcorn blossoms off Jack Horner and grind them through a sieve into a container. You let the pollen in the container dry for a day or so, then you take a mascara brush (or your finger) and you brush Jack Horner's pollen onto the stigma of each of the blossoms on Victoria Sykes.

That's the extent of the actual cross-breeding, which is a human-controlled version of what the bees do. As spring continues, Victoria Sykes will bloom into flower and then set fruit. The flesh of the fruit on the tree is that of the Victoria Sykes variety, no different than what grew on that tree last year or the year before that. The seed surrounded by the flesh is the hybridized thing, and that's what you care about if you're the breeder. Once the fruit matures, you pick it and extract all the pits. You germinate the pits (which now represent the hybrid Jack Horner × Victoria Sykes) and then hope for seedlings. Hybrids are stubborn, though, so many pits won't sprout. Some will, and you plant those. Of those you plant, many won't grow over the first year. Of those, only a small number will bud, and many that bud won't set fruit the following year or the year after that. Of those that set fruit in the second and third years, many won't have fruit that eats well or grows large enough or has enough color.

Let's say you haven't yet given up all hope, so you decide there's one particularly successful variety you want to evaluate some more. Your next step is to asexually propagate the variety—to clone it—by cutting off foot-long sticks from the tree's branches. This is called budwood. You take the budwood from the seedling and you graft it onto fully grown, disease-resistant rootstock. To graft, you slice a flap into the bark of the rootstock, then insert a stick of budwood down inside the flap. You glue or tape the flap closed. You do this several times on one rootstock, and then you repeat the process on however many other trees you want to have for evaluation. That budwood will grow into branches, and the next year, when these trees show fruit, the fruit that grows will be that hybrid offspring of Jack Horner and Victoria Sykes. You'll continue to evaluate the fruit—at this point, you'll assign it a code so that you can track your evaluations—and if it has some characteristics that make it an improvement over what you've been working with in your breeding program, maybe you'll begin crossing with it, too. If it seems like something really special—something that's got flavor, size, durability, something that's farmer friendly—you may select it for the cream of the crop to show on the Wednesday fruit tours. If all has gone well to this point, you're five to seven years out from when you made the original cross between Jack Horner and Victoria Sykes.

Like so many Californians, Floyd Zaiger was born somewhere else: in Nebraska, in 1926. His German father and his Danish mother had moved there from Iowa after it had become clear that neither of their families would welcome having the other in it. The Dust Bowl forced the Zaigers to move back to Iowa the year after Floyd finished kindergarten. They fell in with his mother's people, who ran big cattle and corn farms. The ragweed got so bad in Iowa that his mother's eyesight and hearing started to fail. So for several years she would go for part of the year to Oregon to stay with Floyd's father's sister and her family. Floyd had two sisters and five brothers, and when their mother left for Oregon, they would all be farmed out to aunts and uncles. Once the ragweed had settled, his mother would return from out west and round them all up. Finally, on Floyd's thirteenth birthday, his parents took the children to Oregon to stay. It was 1939, the year Hitler took Poland and Steinbeck published *The Grapes of Wrath*. The Zaigers lived in Floyd's aunt's house, where there were already two families living. They farmed cauliflower and strawberries, and Floyd occasionally worked pulling onions, thousands of acres of which were grown in the area. He went to school in a one-room building where, because he was not the only Floyd in the classroom but the one whose last name was German, people started calling him Fritz. (That's how he still signs the Christmas cards he and Betty send to friends.)

The Zaigers were poor, but they were better off than they'd

been in Iowa, and it was Floyd's job to take fifty cents into town every week and buy a hog's head. The family didn't own a car, and town was five miles if you went along the road, three if you went across the pastures. The butcher would put just one wire through the hog's snout, with no wrapping around the head. Floyd had to hoist it up with the wire, which always cut into his hands. But if he got the head dirty on the way home, there was trouble from his father. So to keep the head clean, he mapped out every tree stump across the pastures so that he could safely set the hog's head down to rest his hands. He'd get the head home—clean—and they'd split it and eat the brains, then have head cheese sandwiches for school. That was the routine.

Floyd's three older brothers all went to war. Of them, only one returned unscathed; Roy was killed in Italy, and Doliver was shot up and sent to recuperate at a hospital in Modesto, where Floyd's mother soon moved to look after him. Floyd was drafted late in the war and sent to San Luis Obispo for basic training. When he had leave time, he'd hitchhike up to Modesto to visit his brother and mother. By the time Floyd got shipped off to Japan, the war had wound down. He got out of the service a few months later and because he had nothing to keep him in Oregon, he moved to Modesto, too. He heard that a neighbor with a small carpentry business was looking for another set of hands. The neighbor couldn't go to the union; if you went to the union, the man said, you'd end up with somebody who only did roofs, or only did siding. "I need somebody who can do roofs, who can do siding, who can dig ditches if that's what we need to do." He offered Floyd $1.25 an hour, which was good money then. The union found out about it, though, after Floyd's first day, and so he didn't work a second one. The only other job Floyd could find was shoveling chicken manure at Foster Farms (which has since grown to become one of the largest poultry producers in the United States). At the time, Floyd drove an old Ford that wouldn't start unless you pushed it. It was light enough to push pretty easily, though, so when he needed gas, he'd dip half a block off the main road and roll over to the Dave Wilson Nursery.

The nursery was in the plant business, of course, but in order to justify the expense of having someone sit in the front office all day, they'd installed one gas pump out front so that whoever was working would have something to keep him busy during the lulls. Floyd would stop in for gas and chat with whoever was working the pump. That person was often John Wynne, who was the young son-in-law of Dave Wilson, the founder of the nursery. Wynne had just finished school and was close to taking over the nursery business. He and Floyd shared a love of fishing and hunting, and they became good friends.

School was something Floyd had been thinking about himself. In 1947, he gave notice at the chicken farm and started taking classes at the junior college in Modesto. A semester later, wanting to study plant physiology, he transferred to the University of California, Davis, which had been set up in 1905 as the farming outpost for the University of California system. (Until 1959, Davis wasn't formally recognized as an official campus and instead was called the "University Farm.") During Floyd's sophomore year at Davis, he met Betty, who was working as a bookkeeper at Woolworth's. They made plans to get married at the beginning of Floyd's junior year. That summer, they didn't see much of each other, though, because Floyd and his brother had applied for and been awarded a government contract to work up in the Sierra Nevadas clearing wild currants and gooseberries, which had been identified as hosts for a tree-killing fungus called white pine blister rust. Floyd and his brother would pack a mule with supplies for a week, go up there and do the clearing work, then come back down to Modesto to resupply for another week or so. They camped in a tent alongside a creek and before they came out of the woods each time, they'd catch a bunch of trout to take to their mother. It was a good job, because up there in the woods, there was nowhere to spend the money they were earning. The bad thing about it was that, as government contract work, it took forever to get paid. So Floyd came out of the woods a broke groom. But Betty had eighty dollars that she had saved from her job, enough for their first month's rent in Davis, where they lived out in a trailer amid the ducks and chicken pens that belonged to the landlord.

After finishing at Davis, Floyd was supposed to go to work at Shell, but the company suddenly cut back; the guy who had assured Floyd a job called and said, "Hey, even I've got to move back to Illinois." Floyd found a job teaching classes at the community college in Modesto. He and Betty rented a house in town next to Muni 9, the city golf course. But having lived on a farm for most of his life, Floyd felt anxious being crammed in there among his neighbors, hearing their conversations at night through the walls. After a year or so, he and Betty looked around for something they could afford. Eventually, they found a crumbling two-and-a-half acre plant nursery on the outskirts of town. It had been bought to sell off inventory, and the windows and doors of the small home and greenhouses were kicked out, weeds growing out the tops of the roofs, which were on the verge of collapse anyway. Instead of tearing the greenhouses down, they decided to fix them up. They jacked up the greenhouses, put in new windows, and repainted the place. Floyd was teaching full-time, but since he had the greenhouses, he decided to put his degree to good use. In his spare time, he started dabbling with azaleas and rhododendrons, trying to breed more heat resistance so that the plants could endure the hot Modesto summers. It was 1953. Floyd was twenty-seven.

With every cross they made, they'd get anywhere from fifty to one hundred seeds, most of which would grow into viable plants. Because the azaleas were purely ornamental and because they were growing the plants to sell directly (as opposed to selling seed to growers), they didn't have to worry about many of the issues that would later plague them as fruit breeders. If a seedling's flowers were pink, they'd call it a "pink" azalea. If the flowers were red, it was a "red" azalea. At that point, just about everything they grew was as good as anything else on the market, so they could try to sell their inventory even as they were still selecting for exceptional stuff to use in their nascent breeding program.

One day, an old classmate of Floyd's stopped by with his boss to take a look around. The boss's name was Fred Anderson and he was a mid-career fruit breeder who would eventually become known as the Father of the Modern Nectarine. Before going out on his own, Anderson had apprenticed with the most famous of plant breeders, Luther Burbank. And now, at Zaiger's, Anderson liked what he saw. Azaleas, nectarines, labradoodles: It didn't matter what you were breeding, only that you had the touch. And Floyd seemed to have the touch. Anderson offered Floyd a job as his second breeder, and Floyd took it; he quit his teaching job, hired a couple to move in and look after the azaleas and rhododendrons, and packed up his young family to move them the sixty miles south to Le Grand. He was given the responsibility with the other breeder of walking through the orchards to determine which of the selections were worth keeping around. Each of them was on his own in making all the selections, and there was very little in the way of training. Anderson had been running his own operation for more than twenty years, so there was plenty of fruit to choose from. They got started very early in the morning, and when Anderson came to the field at half past nine each morning, Floyd and the other breeder handed over their lists of selections that had looked good enough for Anderson to review himself. At the time, Floyd felt like he was being given too much responsibility. His only real experience was with azaleas, and most of the genetics work he'd done in college had to do with dairy cows. What did he know about fruit? What was he supposed to be looking for? What if he missed something? Sometimes, it seemed like Anderson himself didn't know what he was looking for. One day, he'd stop in front of one of the trees Floyd had selected, look it over, and say, "I don't know what you see in *that*." Then, the next day, he'd stop at the same variety, wonder why it wasn't on the list, and say, "Man, that is *beautiful!*"

"I didn't always appreciate it at the time," Floyd said one

morning, as we were walking around checking blossoms, "but looking back, I realize that it couldn't have been any better. It was such a golden opportunity to work for Fred. When he started, there wasn't a carload of nectarines shipped out of California. And by the time he died, there were more nectarines being shipped than peaches."

Most of what Floyd worked on did involve nectarines, but Anderson also kept hounding him to start a hybridizing project with figs. "To his knowledge nobody had ever done anything with figs, and he kept saying to me, 'Man, you'll be the first, so everything you do will look great!'" (Anderson may have been on to something. One of the discipline's classic texts is Jules Janick and James Moore's multivolume *Fruit Breeding*. The chapter on figs they included in their original edition was dropped for the 1996 edition because nothing worth noting had happened in the field for so long.) Nectarines intrigued Floyd, but he was unenthused by figs. And after a season in Le Grand, Floyd was beginning to feel a little bit like a third wheel. The other breeder there had been working with Anderson for years and they behaved like an old married couple, always bickering about something or another.

Meanwhile, things were not going well back in Modesto. Floyd wasn't happy with the family that was looking after the place. When he could, he'd go back on the weekends to check on things. One weekend, he stopped to pick up the mail and noticed an electric bill in the family's name that had a different address on it. Floyd went to investigate and saw that the family had a second place where they stashed the plants they were stealing from the Zaiger greenhouses. Realizing he couldn't keep both jobs going, Floyd left Anderson at the end of the season and moved the family back to Modesto. Floyd remembers the day they returned. He was driving the family in an old car, with all their belongings stuffed into the cattle stalls of a trailer he was pulling. There was a train that ran down the middle of Highway 99 then, and he kept pace with the train, stopping at all the same traffic lights.

"The conductor kept looking down at us. And finally we were stopped at one light, and he looked down at me and he yelled, 'Howdy sharecropper! When'd you get in?'"

Back in Modesto, the Zaigers took to the plant nursery business full time. For the first several months, it seemed to rain every day. There were no customers and there was no money. Things got so bad that Floyd and Betty started taking plants to chain stores like Safeway and to gas stations along the highway. They'd grow the plants in one-gallon cans, stick them in the greenhouse to bring them into bloom, then pull colored foil over the cans to make them look nice. The idea was to put them in the stores and get some impulse buys. They sold each plant to the stores for forty-five cents, and they guaranteed the sale, provided the store didn't sell the plants for more than ninety-nine cents a can. They tried to put them as close as possible to the bread stand, on the theory that people still had to buy bread, rain or no rain.

The first couple of stores they got into sold every single plant, and soon they were delivering plants all over northern California. A few days a week, Betty would take the delivery truck to Fresno and Sacramento with the two youngest children, Leith and Grant, in tow. On the other days, Floyd made the San Francisco runs. It rained so much that some of the underpasses flooded, and the highway authorities had to plank out in the field around the underpasses to keep the highways open.

Some stores weren't immediately receptive to the plants. Floyd remembered going to see the manager of one local grocery. "He said, 'Azaleas? Azaleas? What the hell are azaleas?' I said, 'Come out and let me show you.' I brought him out and raised the curtain on the truck and some ladies walked by and said, 'What do you want for those?' I said, 'Ninety-nine cents.' And boy, they started grabbing them and he gave me an order right then." As they branched out to more and more stores, they ran into the same pattern: It was hard to get in to see a manager, much less convince him to buy anything. But once you could show him some sales, he was glad to see you. The bottom line was that you had to make the buyers some money. That was true in azaleas, and it would be true in stone fruit.

Even as the Zaigers spent all their daylight hours tending to the ornamental nursery business, Floyd was having a hard time forgetting about fruit. During his two seasons with Fred Anderson, Floyd often says, he had been "bitten by the dreaded disease of fruit breeding." From his experiences with Anderson, with whom he would stay friends until Anderson's death, Floyd knew that fruit breeding was an old man's game whose progress was best measured on a long clock. It was a trade best not dabbled in, something you had to treat like a calling. Stone fruit required years of work before you could even tell if a variety had real potential. A few years would go by as a breeder made selections from his crosses. And then another few would go by as he evaluated the selections. With luck he'd have something worth patenting and releasing as a variety right off the bat, but several more years would pass before any growers would see fruit from the variety. In most cases, once a variety really took hold among growers and the royalties started coming in, the breeder would already be two-thirds through the period of patent protection. "Disease" is the best word to describe what causes someone to become a private fruit breeder. No well person would pursue it unless it was on somebody else's dime.

Knowing that he had a long road ahead of him, Floyd was eager to get his own fruit breeding operation going as early as possible. Whenever anyone asks how he started, he tells a little story, always pacing it like a "man-walks-into-a-bar" joke: "Well, I went in to my wife," he'll say as the setup, "and I said, 'Betty, this breeding is going to be a long-range project.' She said okay. 'I think it will take twelve to fifteen years for the first income to come back.' She said okay." There's always a pause here, as his face opens into a wide smile—it's a short joke. "And then I was pretty close. Twelve years later, I brought her a check for two hundred fifty dollars." This last bit comes across as the punch line, but it also happens to be roughly true.

2

Across the street from the Dinuba headquarters of Family Tree Farms, a golf community called Ridge Creek was in the works. According to the brochure, the development would have four hundred new homes built in "three separate golf course neighborhoods." The course itself would have the longest par five in California (653 yards) and the largest driving range west of the Rockies. For now, it was just a flat expanse of dirt. I could see bulldozers working trenches in the distance.

The parking spot closest to the front doors at Family Tree is reserved for the "Best Grower." The privilege of parking there rotates among David Jackson, his two sons Rick and Daniel, and his son-in-law Andy Muxlow. (It's generally first come, first served.) Each of them owns his own ranch, and collectively they feed into the packing facility and sales company that is Family Tree Farms. While David is Family Tree's main strategist and figurehead who seeks out new fruits and evangelizes on behalf of flavor, Rick spends most of his time in the orchard, Andy oversees the marketing department, and Daniel runs the packing shed.

It was Daniel who joined his dad to meet me. By way of introduction, David said, "At the end of every season we say that things could be better next year. Well, this is the official beginning of next year."

It's often said that if you've seen one packing shed, you've seen them all. And while it's true that the underlying order is the same from shed to shed—fruit comes in, gets sorted and put in a box, and then goes out—it's also true that packing sheds are defined by their little differences. Think, if you can bear it, of two separate floors in a big office building and how one sea of cubicles can seem entirely different from another because of the height, orientation, and texture of the dividers, the color of the walls, the lighting in the rooms, and the ring tones of the phone system. Packing sheds are distinct in that same way. While they're all essentially big hangars filled with similar component parts, each hangar *feels* different. One cavernous packing shed I visited was tinted in a dusky orange glow that somehow fit the mood of the overall company. Another was so tight—the space managed so efficiently—that it felt like a submarine control room. The main floor of the Family Tree shed was bright and airy. Two open bays in the north and east walls let in plenty of light and the scale of the shed was well proportioned for the machinery that filled it. It wasn't so large that you felt tiny inside it; nor was it so snug that you felt trapped.

The shed was still empty at this time of year. In order to keep the machines running and the revenue coming in year-round, many packers run contraseasonal crops—mostly citrus—in the winter. Family Tree, though, is a pure summer-fruit operation, so the shed was still in mothballs.

We walked around to the open bay on the shed's north side, where most of the fruit comes in on flatbed trucks from the orchards. Instead of the industry standard bin packing, in which fruit is picked into individual totes and then dumped by the pickers into a big hamper, Family Tree picks its fruit into shallow, stackable pallets. Because of the fragility of stone fruit, there are very few things growers and packers can do to mechanize their way to greater efficiency. Just as you can't shake a plum off the tree like a walnut, you can't run a plum through a packing shed like a carrot, virtually untouched by human hands. Still, you could make small improvements here and there, and one such piece of equipment the Jacksons had invested in was a pallet flipper that quickly dumped the fruit from each pallet onto the conveyor that would take it down the line.

"When you have humans loading pallets, they drop one," Daniel said. "But the machine always sets the fruit down in the most gentle way. Plus, the machine doesn't complain, and it doesn't get backaches."

Once a box was filled, it was moved to a holding area directly behind the packing line. The boxes were stacked onto pallets, and full pallets were tagged with a bar code and then picked up by forklifts which carried them into the pre-cooling room. Here, neighboring rows of pallets were covered in a tarp in order to force cold air into the boxes and cool the fruit down to 33 to 34 degrees Fahrenheit. This near-freezing temperature stopped the ripening process, so that the fruit would firm up and last longer for the coming journey to whichever distant point it was bound. This usually took five to six hours, though it could take longer if the fruit was especially warm. Once the fruit was cooled down to just above freezing, the pallets were either loaded onto trucks or moved into cold storage to await shipment. It was standard practice in just about every packing shed to operate on a "first in, first out" basis. The forklifts were equipped with scanners, so they could easily run through the bar codes to find the load that had been in cold storage the longest. If all went well during the harvest season, a packer's cold storage area wouldn't get so full that he had to worry about losing pallets in the system, but there were some years—2004, for example—when a lot of the fruit that went into cold storage never made it onto a truck. It sat and sat and sat until the fruit was good for nothing.

As we were leaving the packing shed, I noticed a dozen or so flattened boxes stuck to the wall above the second packing line. Each box had a different label, among them Flavor Safari (Family Tree's premium label for pluots) and Great White (a shark-festooned label for their white-fleshed peaches and nectarines). These were Family Tree's most common labels, though they used more, depending on what the buyer wanted and where the fruit was going. And in just over a decade, they had gone from two box styles to several dozen.

The boxes were stored in one corner of the shed, where they were assembled as needed and then hooked onto a conveyor that ran above the packing line and then curved back behind the packing stations. Each packing station had a little screen on which the packer could see the variety she was packing. (All the packers are women and all the palletizers are men.) She could then turn around and find the box right there on the conveyor.

Keeping up with all the different box styles and having to

slow down and stop the line to make adjustments was inefficient, but ultimately it made sense given that Family Tree had positioned itself as a high-end specialty supplier. "We're doing fruit where we've got to keep the bloom on," Daniel said, "so we can't go super-slamming things into walls at full speed. It might cost us ten cents a box more to do all this, but if it means that we get paid two more dollars a box, then that makes a lot of sense, doesn't it? To be quite honest, these boxes are what's kept us in the ball game."

For others, it's what drove them out. Or, in Rod Milton's case, almost drove him out. This time of year was when he used to dust off his own packing line. It was a modest line, a line that a few people could handle—a far cry from the hangar at Family Tree. He usually had to spend a few weeks doing a tune-up, tightening screws and replacing belts, but it had been worthwhile because it had given him more control over what he packed and how he packed it.

Then came the bloodbath of 2004. After looking over his costs, Rod had decided that the only way he could stay in the deal would be to hook up with a commercial packer.

The main factor in his decision was the great proliferation of box styles. While having dozens of different box styles did make larger growers like Family Tree less efficient, they were generally able to absorb the extra costs because of their size. For a grower of Rod's size, though, having to stop the packing line to change to a different box was brutal for his labor costs. Even worse, he had to order and store all these different boxes just in case he needed them, and often, he'd just end up with a big stack of obsolete boxes.

"You end up giving all the money to the box company," he said when I went to see him after touring Family Tree's shed. Though the box issue had been a problem for the past ten to fifteen years, Rod had tried to manage the problem as well as possible. But in the aftermath of 2004, he had realized that he was never going to be able to keep up with all the different pack styles that buyers were now demanding. It would cost him too much time and too much money to do so—time and money he didn't have.

Given the proximity of Ballantine and the fact that his brother, Rick, was its head of grower services, David Albertson's company was a natural fit for Rod. His first two seasons with Ballantine had gone well enough. He'd had to make some slight changes to the way he did things. For example, when he'd done his own packing, he'd grown several of his plums for the export market, which was more tolerant of (and in some cases actually preferred) smaller fruit. For those plums, he was usually able to get them all in two picks: The first pick cleaned out the top and sides of the tree while the second one took care of the inside fruit. Ballantine, however, planned on shipping more of Rod's fruit to markets in the United States, where consumers preferred larger fruit. This meant that Rod now needed to do three or four picks of those varieties instead of two. More picks meant higher labor costs.

The other issue was psychological. After decades of pretty much calling his own shots, Rod was now having to coordinate with other people. He wasn't constitutionally opposed to that; he just wasn't used to all the *talk*. Given all that, Rod was still happy with the arrangement. He'd had two good years of sales with Ballantine. Plus, not having to pack his own stuff gave him more time to focus on being a good grower.

In stone fruit, what happens during the summer is mostly because of what happened during the winter and spring, and many things happened in the first several months of 2007 that would be important during the growing season to come. On New Year's Day, the minimum wage had gone up fifty cents in California. Growers would be paying more for labor, assuming they could get it. With the Mexican border tightening and the immigration bill stalled in Congress, many growers feared that field workers would be hard to come by in the first place. (Just several months earlier, California pear growers had lost millions of dollars in fruit that had gone unharvested because there was no one to pick it.)

In the first six weeks of the year, there hadn't been much snow in the Sierras, leaving many to suspect that water would be an issue in some places, as it had been for several years. Every fruit grower I met seemed to know how many new homes had been built in the past couple of years (nearly one hundred and fifty thousand in Fresno County alone), how much water they sucked up (water for five houses would irrigate four acres of fruit), and where the homeowners' priorities would be when the water dried up (flush toilet vs. eat plums).

Because of the January freeze, the bloom in February was off the charts. The white plum blossoms and pink and red peach and nectarine blossoms were growing on top of each other, almost like double flowers. "Generally when you see that, you don't get a lot of nectar in the flower," Rod said. "I think there's just not a lot of vitality in the flowers and so the bees aren't working them as hard."

There was also the shortage of bees to worry about. Whole colonies were dying off, and no one really knew why. It had led to a scramble among fruit growers, who were competing with other farmers across the West for hives, especially California almond growers. Almond trees need lots of bees for pollination, and as more and more growers were moving from fruits to nuts, bees were already in high demand. With fewer bees than normal (and with less active bees), pollination would be light. When pollination was light, fruit that needed another variety to pollenize it generally wouldn't set as well. Since most plums did need a pollenizer, Rod anticipated that the plum set would be light. (To help with this, he'd been out doing some bloom-time pruning to shake the trees and help the pollen fall out.) A light set across the board was often a good thing, because it meant a lower volume of fruit would hit the market later in the summer, keeping prices higher. Of course, it all depended on the set of *your* trees, Rod emphasized. "Everyone wants to have a heavy set on his fruit but a light set on everybody else's. Last year, we were very short as an industry, but it was a really good year for me."

To illustrate how generally bad conditions could work in one person's favor, he showed me a framed bill of sale dated June 15, 1995. It was a receipt for 958 boxes of Blackamber plums, which Rod had picked on June 13 and 14. On June 15, at three o'clock in the afternoon, as his Blackambers were on the way to the harbor in San Pedro, a hail storm had hit the southern San Joaquin and destroyed much of the Valley's remaining plum crop. Rod's Blackambers had been some of the only Blackambers left in California, and the salesman he was working with had been able to get five times the normal domestic box price from a buyer in Taiwan. In that one sale, Rod had made half of what he might have made in a normal year.

The epilogue to the story is even more interesting. Usually export sales were kind of "send the fruit and hope for the best" deals, with the sales company paying freight and taking responsibility for the fruit until it arrived in Taiwan. The salesman would nail down a price per box, get it on the boat, and then renegotiate once the fruit arrived at its destination. But since so many Blackambers had been destroyed by hail, the Asian buyer had wanted to lock down the price and guarantee the sale, so he had assumed the freight costs and signed off before the fruit was loaded onto the boat for Taiwan. Good thing, too: one day into the trip across the Pacific, the compressor had broken down. By the time the fruit had arrived in Taiwan, it was rotten.

Broken compressors were always possible, but hail was more likely. Having been burned too many times by it, the big growers had installed hail cannons that shot bursts of air into the sky to try to disrupt any clouds looming over their orchards. The cannons were going off all spring.

3

Rod had invited me to tag along to the California Tree Fruit Agreement's first educational symposium, which was held on a Wednesday in late February at the downtown Fresno convention center. I signed in at the registration table and shuffled around, looking for a familiar face. Just about everyone who was anyone in California stone fruit was here at the symposium or had sent a proxy. As a rule, you could look at the shoes (muddy vs. shiny) and shirts (button-down vs. point collar) to distinguish the growers from the marketers and the CTFA staff. There were lots of cell phones clipped to belt loops, and very few women. I spotted Rod just as everyone was filing into a windowless conference room for the morning session. We sat in the back row, next to the field manager at David Jackson's Family Tree Farms.

The first speaker was Louis Ng, the CTFA's representative in China. In 2006, a new trade agreement allowed growers in the San Joaquin to ship plums to mainland China for the first time. (In turn, growers from certain regions of China could ship their pears to the United States.) Traditionally, Asian-bound

California plums were shipped to Taiwan and made it onto the mainland from there. The direct relationship with China was a huge opening for plum growers. "There's been an eight percent increase in fresh fruit consumption in China, and the [fruit-growing] industry there is not really mature. There's no infrastructure," Ng said to the rapt crowd. "It holds a lot of promise for you." Lots of nods in the audience.

But, Ng said quietly, there was a small window of opportunity. American plums were generally much more expensive than Chinese plums, he said. There were certain areas—Shanghai, for example—where they could market California plums, but in general they were still a luxury good. Growers in China, meanwhile, were planting a lot of the same varieties as California had and were already exporting to Hong Kong, Japan, Pakistan, and other places. "Once the logistics system improves, China could be a major competitor to you, a real threat." There was shuffling and coughing around me. Then, Ng ended on a glass-half-full note. The window was small, but there was time, ten years maybe, during which California could carve out a section of the market, even as the Chinese plum industry grew.

Next up was Paul Stuart, a "senior produce category merchant" from Wegman's, a mid-size upscale chain with stores in the mid-Atlantic and New England. It was a dream store for fruit growers. In an era when most stores' produce section employees couldn't tell the difference between a Fuji and a Granny Smith, Stuart was urging stone fruit to go the way of the apple and try to market more varieties by name. People in the audience, who were used to the black and red plum ghettos, traded looks: *What did he say?* (Many Wegman's locations keep refractometers in the store so produce managers can show customers the Brix levels of various fruits.) Stuart said that one of the chain's cofounders, Danny Wegman, was fond of saying that the peach was the "single most difficult product to get right" in the store.

Stuart was trying to play a short video about the opening of a new Wegman's branch, but the sound wasn't working. As we watched absurdly enthusiastic people mouth silently at the camera, several growers around me took advantage of the lull and got in a quick nap. When the video's sound came on, someone was blurting, "I am so excited! I am never cooking dinner again!" Stuart started the video over. It was surprisingly good. The store's produce section looked spacious and grand, the fruit stacked in neat towers. I found myself thinking: *If I were a plum grower, that's where I'd want my fruit to end up.*

After the video, Stuart whipped through a brief powerpoint presentation, covering recent sales figures, the importance of food safety, and the rise of organics. One of the last slides read:

What will drive sales?
Taste-Taste-Taste

Stuart looked out at the assembled crowd and said simply, "We've got to have the best varieties out there and they have to be picked at the best times. We need hand-picked, ripe fruit. We need more flavor! We cannot offer the perfect fruit if you don't set the table for us." There was big applause. That hardly sounded like "big, red, hard."

At lunch, I sat between Rod and a fruit-growing neighbor of his; their families went way back. "In the day, my family traded his family a pony for a cocker spaniel," Rod said. "Or maybe it was the other way around." The keynote speaker at lunch was supposed to be California's Secretary of Agriculture, A. G. Kawamura, but he had had to cancel at the last minute, so one of his deputies had come. Over steak with scalloped potatoes, green beans, and carrots, we watched his slide show about the various diseases and pests that could wreck California agriculture—seemingly at any minute. The Asian Longhorn Beetle. The Oriental Fruit Fly. Citrus canker. Then dessert.

I went to a couple of panels after lunch and then sat in on a presentation by the CTFA's marketing people. For the past few years, the industry had been working with an outside consumer research consultant named John Lundeen. He had worked with, among others, the California Strawberry Commission, the American Lamb Council, and the Almond Board of California. He was about to start a new job as the executive director of market research for the National Cattlemen's Beef Association. This was his CTFA swan song.

Lundeen started by talking about the work he'd done with the almond industry in the mid-1990s. During the first focus groups he had conducted about almonds, he kept hearing people say that they made you fat, were bad for your heart, and increased your cholesterol. In response, the almond industry had underwritten some nutritional studies. One thing they had discovered was that almonds were high in vitamin E, an antioxidant that was perceived as being good for your heart. From that small starting point, they had begun to talk to nutritionists about almonds and eventually, the message had morphed from "almonds are bad for you" to "you can have some almonds every day and get good cholesterol" to "eat an ounce to an ounce and a half of almonds a day."

At the same time, they had been conducting consumer research to figure out who the target audience for almonds was. In the mid-1990s, few Americans were just snacking on almonds. Most of the almonds we ate in the United States were *in* other things—primarily candy bars, cereals, and ice creams—and so the industry's marketing had been pushing the message that "almonds made other food better." Gradually, though, Lundeen had started to see focus groups populated with women who carried "little bags of almonds in their purses. They were starting to take almonds on the road with them. They were starting to pack almonds in their husbands' lunches, because their husbands had cholesterol problems. So there was this shift. Almonds didn't just make *food* better. They made *life* better."

Though the challenges facing stone fruit weren't the same ones that almonds had faced, a similar sequence had been set in motion for peaches, plums, and nectarines. First, the nutritional angle: Lundeen mentioned recent research that has shown plums—specifically red-fleshed plums—to have some really powerful antioxidant qualities. "So you're starting to get a little bit of a story here. It's a story that you can start to approach the dietician with, the food writer with." (When you start reading plum-as-antioxidant stories in the food section of your local paper, remember Lundeen.)

Then came the consumer research, for which Lundeen and his team had followed consumers through the grocery store while they were shopping. Here's what they found about your relationship with plums: If you are that earnest blank known as

Average Consumer, then you think of plums as "a little more adult, a little more gourmet" than peaches or nectarines. You prefer them as a midafternoon snack, something to tide you over until dinner. You like a plum that fits in the palm of your hand, somewhere between the size of a cue ball and a baseball. Anything larger than a baseball and you start to worry about waste. Anything racquetball-size or smaller, and the pit-to-fruit ratio seems too high. While you're comfortable with pretty much any dark plum—red, black, or purple—a green plum tends to confuse you because you're not sure how to tell when they're ripe.

What happens when you get a really great plum? According to Lundeen's research, you tell all your friends about it. "Word of mouth just takes off," he said. "This one woman in Colorado said, 'My mother called from Florida to tell me to get into the store because the plums were really good.' So it's wildfire, okay? When they get a good piece of fruit, people tell their friends and you're promoting consumption." And when you buy a bland, tasteless plum? You wait two to three weeks to buy another one. Why two to three weeks? Because you associate that plum with the plums it came in with—if it's bad, they must all be bad—and two to three weeks is how long you assume it will take for that batch to work its way out of the store. And who do you blame for the bad plum? According to Lundeen, you don't blame the plum industry (probably because you don't know that there is one) and you don't blame the store. Mostly, you just blame yourself. You don't know how to pick a good one. You're uninformed. You're just wasting money. And you don't want to make the same mistake again, so you wait a few weeks.

Apparently, this scenario had been happening way too often for way too long. The result, as Ballantine's Rick Milton and John Kaprielian had shown me on their wall charts, was that over the course of twenty years the volume of California peaches, plums, and nectarines had dropped twenty-five percent.

In 1984, Americans ate on average one and a half pounds of plums per person. By 2004, we were down to a pound of plums each per year. (Fresh apple consumption, on the other hand, was nearly eighteen and a half pounds per person in 2004.) Lundeen was touching on this indirectly when he suggested that the industry's priority should be on figuring out how to inspire more repeat sales. Unlike almonds, the issue wasn't necessarily getting more people to eat plums, he said. It was getting people who already ate plums to eat them more often. To help the industry figure out who was already buying plums, Lundeen and his group had worked on identifying a target audience.

"One group we called Generation Starbucks. We said, 'Let's look at these younger consumers and see if they're a fertile group to sell peaches, plums, and nectarines to.'" Short answer: no. They were too busy, their lives too hectic.

But a second group was more promising. They called this group the Summer Passionates. "These are people who think that summer is the most special time of the year," said Lundeen. "It's the time they do what they totally love in life. They exercise more. They walk, hike, mountain bike. They spend time with their families. Summer Passionates are people who just love the activities associated with summer." If you're thinking, *Well, damn, that must be about half the population*, then you're not too far off. "We found that there are about one hundred and eleven million Summer Passionates out there. And guess what? They're buying a lot of fruit. You know, they're filling up picnic baskets and when you fill up your picnic basket, you're filling it up with fruit." It got even better. "We looked at another target group we called Super Moms and Dads. Guess what? Of the seventy-two million Super Moms and Dads, forty-six million of them are also Summer Passionates. So it's also about these parents who are trying to teach their children about nutrition. That's the same parent who's going to take the kids to do summer activities."

There were a lot of smiles in the room after Lundeen's presentation, and the good cheer lasted into mid-spring. Most everything was going well for stone fruit growers in California. The strong bloom and warm weather meant fruit quality was probably going to be excellent. On top of that, the bee shortage might lighten the set a little bit, which could help keep the overall volume of fruit down and maybe keep the market up. The CTFA had solid marketing in place for 2007—watch out, Summer Passionates!—and over the course of the season, the organization had decided to highlight plums, to make 2007 the year of the plum.

In mid-March, Rod started thinning his trees. The act of thinning was what made the coming season begin to feel real to Rod. Each grower had a different take on when the season really "started." For David Jackson, it was when the chill hours had been met and the trees started showing blossoms. For others, it wouldn't really start until they'd picked the first piece of fruit. For Rod, though, thinning was when you had to take a deep breath and jump. In early April, he sent me a report: "Rapid growth in stuff now, visible day to day . . . Some folks ride bulls, hang glide, race motorcycles, and chase tornados. I just farm fruit and it's about all the drama I can handle!"

Though the set on plums and pluots did indeed look to be a little light as of mid-spring, the weather was cooperating with growers. Plenty of sun and not much rain meant lots of sugar was being developed in the fruit. If all went well from here, growers could be looking at an overall crop whose volume was down but which ate well across the board—a recipe for a profitable season.

4

L
UTHER BURBANK WENT to California for many reasons, but he went mostly because he was young and it was
California. Burbank was born in 1849 in central Massachusetts.
His family's home in Lancaster was twenty miles due west of
Concord and within the intellectual shadow cast by Thoreau
and Emerson, so Burbank was exposed early on not only to the
natural world around him and the ersatz natural world that was
farming, but also to the ideas about the natural world that were
shaping that time. When he was nineteen, Burbank read Darwin's newly published *Variation of Animals and Plants Under Domestication* and his fate was sealed. He bought seventeen acres of
land near his family's home and began growing vegetables for
the competitive Boston market. He paid constant attention to
which of his plants grew the fastest and healthiest. As he harvested his vegetables, noted Peter Dreyer, Burbank's most recent biographer, he tagged those plants that "bore more or bigger
produce than ordinary, or fruit that was of superior quality, or
ripened earlier or later than average." These superior plants were
the ones he selected to take seeds from to grow the next year.

Then, he did the same thing with the following season's crop, in each cycle improving his stock. As he continued to select out the best and most interesting specimens, he began crossing different plants, and his life as a breeder was under way.

Burbank's first big success (probably the greatest of all his successes) was the Burbank potato. The mid-century potato blight had nearly wiped out the plant as a viable crop in Europe and North America, where potato cultivation was then essentially starting from scratch with varieties brought in from Central and South America. The potato had been grown in these southern climes for thousands of years, but the varieties had not improved much; they tended to be small, ugly, and relatively quick to go bad. What was needed, Burbank decided, was "a large, white, fine-grained potato," and so he set out to produce one.

Things didn't start well. He crossed varieties and selected out the best, but none of them was much of an improvement. He considered abandoning his work on the potato, but then, one day, he got lucky and discovered an almost unheard-of seed pod attached to an Early Rose potato, a descendant of the first Central American potatoes brought to the United States in 1851. Burbank planted the twenty-three seeds he got out of the pod and selected two of the resulting potatoes. They were, he later wrote, "as different from the Early Rose as modern beef cattle from the old Texas Longhorns." Burbank began selling his potatoes at market when he was twenty-four years old. The one he called the "Burbank potato" was an immediate hit, and a couple of years later, he sold all his potatoes to a Massachusetts seedsman for $150 and the right to keep ten potatoes for his own use. Later, someone discovered a genetic mutation of the Burbank that had russet skin. It was called the Russet Burbank, and it quickly grew to become the most popular potato in the United States.

In 1875, Burbank took a bundle of clothes, some books, and his ten potatoes, and he set out for California. Immediately upon his arrival (just a few years later than Rod Milton's great grandfather Julius), Burbank encountered the area's fruit, which was, because of the better climate and longer growing season, much larger and more plentiful than in Massachusetts. In a letter to his family, Burbank wrote: "I wish you could see California fruit. I bought a pear in San Francisco, when I thought I was hungry, for five cents. It was so large that I could only eat two thirds of it. I threw the rest away."

Burbank's moving to California when he did was one of those fortuitous historical collisions of a person, time, and place that are hard in retrospect to imagine having been otherwise. He bought some acreage in Santa Rosa and began growing various plants and fruits with the idea of setting up a nursery. Of all the plants he worked with, Burbank was most fascinated by plums; he would later estimate that, with the possible exception of the spineless cactus, he had spent more time working on plums than on anything else.

At the time, most of the plums growing in California were the same European and domesticated American varieties that Burbank would have found at home. A few of these were still hanging around from the former Spanish missions, but most of these European plums had been shipped from nurseries back east, so that the nursery business out west was an extension of what it had been in Massachusetts, even though the terrain and climate of California were very different. In the second half of the nineteenth century, though, Asian immigration was changing the landscape of California. Japan was undergoing the Meiji Restoration that would open up the country after centuries of isolation. One effect of the political changes in Japan was that fruits and vegetables cultivated there could be exported more easily to the United States. In 1870, a man named Hough imported some cuttings of a variety called Botankin. Several years later, a Berkeley nurseryman named John Kelsey sold the first fresh fruit from an American-planted Japanese plum tree. The fruit was probably from Botankin budwood, but a distributor renamed the plums in honor of Kelsey. Meanwhile, an Oaklander named Chabot ordered another Japanese plum—maybe the same Botankin—which he immediately renamed the Chabot.

In Burbank's first nursery catalogue, he lists a handful of Japanese plums, among them the Botan, the Botankio, the Botankio No. 2, and the Chabot. In a later catalogue, he added the Abundance, which was the name he'd given to an open-pollinated selection he'd made from one of the trees he'd bought from either Kelsey or Chabot.

Having seen some interesting results from these Japanese plums that Hough and Chabot had imported, Burbank decided to find some of his own. This decision was inspired partly by the changes he'd noticed in himself since moving to California. He had been a wispy man, but the climate and quality of life out west had unshackled Burbank and invigorated his health. This made him curious to know if California could have the same kind of effect on imported plants. Would a plum tree that had done just okay in Japan really come alive in warmer, sunnier California?

In *How Plants Are Trained to Work for Man*, the eight-volume memoirs he wrote later in his life, Burbank recalled "the precise stimulus" that had led him to look "toward Japan as the probable source of a new race of plums." In a chapter he titled "How the Plum Followed the Potato," Burbank wrote that he'd been poking around the Mercantile Library in San Francisco, when he'd found the journals of an American who'd sailed around the islands of Japan. In the travelogue was a description of a delicious red-fleshed plum the sailor called "the blood plum of Satsuma." Burbank was intrigued by the idea of introducing red flesh into his gene pool. He wanted the blood plum. To get it, he contacted Isaac Bunting, whose family's nursery business had begun in 1820, in Colchester, England. The young Bunting had moved to Japan to hunt for exotic lilies, which the family later popularized in England. Based in Yokohama, Isaac of Japan (as he was called to distinguish him from his grandfather, also named Isaac) agreed to travel south to Satsuma for Burbank. Once there, he was able to track down the blood plum as well as a handful of other red-fleshed plums. In November 1884, Burbank received his first shipment of trees. They were all dead. Undeterred, he contacted Bunting again and asked him to send another batch. This second shipment arrived in December 1885, and as Burbank later reported, "the tiny trees were found in good condition."

There were twelve varieties of plums in the shipment. Of these, Burbank selected two to release as varieties. He named one the Satsuma, and in keeping with a time-honored tradition, he called the other one the Burbank. Both quickly became popular, especially the Burbank, which shipped well enough to hold up from California to the markets back east, and was adaptable enough to be grown in Europe and South Africa. The real value of the Satsuma and Burbank, though, along with some of the other Japanese plums Bunting had sent, would come as parents in the breeding operation that Burbank was getting under way.

Burbank became one of the first breeders to cross Asian plums with native American ones. To describe his work with plums, Burbank invoked a term that was starting to get a lot of play among social scientists as more and more people immigrated to the United States:

> The various plums . . . of the world should be brought together and, as it were, put into one *melting pot* in which a vast number of hereditary tendencies could be combined and recombined . . . Out of the melange would arise new varieties better fitted to meet the old requirements or adapted to meet altogether new requirements . . . My next and all subsequent introductions were from new races produced by crossing and hybridization, combining the heredities of widely varying species and selecting the best from among millions of seedlings. [Author's emphasis]

That kind of language—*melting pot, melange, new races*—betrayed Burbank's having bought into Darwin early on and then not having kept up with the debate over evolution. When the teenaged Burbank read Darwin's *Variation of Animals and Plants Under Domestication,* the evolutionist was still putting forward the idea of pangenesis as the force behind heredity. Pangenesis was an ancient idea that there were particles of inheritance—pangenes—that were shed off the body like dander. These particles were picked up by other bodies and passed through the bloodstream into the reproductive system. The belief explained the influence of environment over inheritance; plants could "pick up" traits through the air, like a common cold, and then pass them down into a new race.

Burbank ran his nursery like a big pangenetic melting pot; his followers portrayed him as a kind of high pagan priest who sang to his plants and believed that they fared best when they were doted upon in a nurturing environment. "The secret of improved plant breeding," he once wrote, "apart from scientific knowledge, is love." Burbank became known as the "wizard of Santa Rosa," favoring the intuitive approach over the analytical, the mystical over the strictly scientific. This was reflected in his grand (and very American) plan to take plums from all over the world and *blend* together their best qualities in an "attempt to produce an ideal plum." He attributed to plums the presumed characteristics of the people who cultivated them. Chinese plums "bore the imprint of the conservatism of the Chinese race." Japanese plums displayed a residual "insularity" from the centuries Japan had spent closed off from the world. European plums exhibited "diversity," Persian plums "nomadism," and American plums "hardiness and variability." Burbank's plan was to take the best varieties available from these "five widely varying geographical territories" and put them on his property in Santa Rosa, where their good qualities "were to be assembled, combined, sifted and selected" to produce that ideal plum.

Though some of his ideas now sound so obviously misguided, he was able to develop an incredible number of lasting plant and fruit varieties, more than eight hundred in all, including spineless cacti, thornless blackberries, giant cherries, and Elephant Garlic. He also released the first "plumcots," which were half-plum and half-apricot. Today, he's best known for the Shasta daisy, the eponymous potato, and the Santa Rosa plum.

He introduced the red-fleshed Santa Rosa in 1907 and it was the closest he was to come to an "ideal plum." The exact parentage of the Santa Rosa is unknown, but it's thought to have been a hybrid of three separate species: *Prunus americana*, *Prunus salicina*, and *Prunus simonii*, otherwise known as the apricot plum. The *simonii* had black skin, red flesh, and a firm texture. It probably originated in northern China, but no one was really sure where it belonged taxonomically. Some considered it an apricot, while others called it a variation of the Japanese plum. Still others thought of it as a natural plum-apricot hybrid, a bridge between the two fruits. Whatever it was, it was definitely in the mix of the Santa Rosa, which quickly became the most popular plum in the world. It was still the most widely grown plum in America as late as 1975.

By the time Burbank introduced the Santa Rosa, Gregor Mendel's laws concerning the inheritance of traits were being rediscovered and absorbed into the scientific community. An Austrian monk, Mendel was interested in the variation of plants, and he spent almost a decade studying peas in the gardens of the monastery where he lived. The result was a paper called "Experiments with Plant Hybridization," in which he laid out some general laws about how characteristics are passed down from parents to children. The paper was published in 1866, but no one paid attention to it until it resurfaced forty years later and became the backbone of modern genetics.

Practically speaking, Burbank mostly ignored the implications of the new hereditary science; his belief in "blending" characteristics was too ingrained in him. Also, his eccentricity extended to his record-keeping, so even if he had realized the implications of Mendel's work on plant breeding, Burbank wouldn't have been able to retrace in detail how certain characteristics had been passed down from one generation of fruit to the next. And in any case, what good would it have done him to rethink the process on which he'd based his entire career? As he later advised a biographer: "Read Darwin first, and gain a full comprehension of the meaning of Natural Selection. Then read the modern Mendelists in detail. But then—go back again to Darwin."

Burbank's refusal to acknowledge the importance of Mendel (not to mention his embrace of eugenics) eventually hurt his reputation among scientists and other plant breeders. But to the public at large, he became as important a figure as his acquaintances Thomas Edison and Henry Ford. Like Edison and Ford, Burbank was famous not only for what he did but for what he came to represent. Just as the name "Ford" spoke to the possibilities of the automobile and "Edison" was shorthand for the innovations of the modern age, "Burbank" was the stand-in for all of man's work in the plant kingdom. More than any one new plant variety Burbank brought into the world, his lasting legacy, one later disciple said, was that "he awakened a universal interest in plant breeding."

Still, as famous as he was, Burbank struggled his entire life to make his breeding operation profitable. Burbank released more than one hundred plums over the course of his life, and just as he did with his eponymous potato and almost every other new variety he developed, Burbank sold the rights to his plums after introducing them. Though he kept the right to continue using a variety in his breeding program, he usually received a one-time fee for the variety itself and had to surrender any future claim on the profits made from its propagation and sale. That, of course, is where the true value of a variety lies, and that Burbank couldn't benefit from the public acceptance of his fruit was a pain he felt more and more as his varieties became known across the world. Toward the end of his life, he acknowledged what Floyd Zaiger would come to realize after being bitten by the dreaded disease of fruit breeding. "Plant improvement of any kind tests purse and patience," Burbank wrote. "But the improvement of tree fruits strains both to the breaking point. Working with vegetables or flowers, it is possible to get valuable improvements well under way in from three to five years—after which, continued selection makes progress more rapid. With tree fruits you have only just begun after a dozen years of crossing, growing, testing, and selecting." Then, he added this weary postscript: "Viewing the work in retrospect I assuredly have no cause to regret that it was undertaken, yet it has been a most laborious task."

★   ★   ★

The chronicles of fruit breeding were already littered with cases who might have had cause to regret the path they had chosen. Take Jacob Moore. His entry in the 1914 edition of Liberty Hyde Bailey's *Standard Cyclopedia of Horticulture* tells a woeful but not uncommon tale: "Moore, Jacob, pomologist, was born at Brighton, New York in 1836. His life work was the development of new fruits, which he produced in large numbers by scientific plant breeding. He was the originator of the Diploma currant, Red Cross currant, Hooker strawberry, Brighton Diana Hamburg and Moore's Diamond grapes, Barr Seckel pear and thousands of other fruits, which have enriched the fruit growers of America many thousands of dollars, but which brought him hardly a sufficient pittance to keep body and soul together."

Or consider the case of Ephraim Bull (whom Paul Collins profiles winningly in his book about losers, *Banvard's Folly*). After struggling for years to breed a grape that could rival the classic European grapes but still withstand the climate and pests of New England, Bull finally pulled from his vines some grapes that seemed worthy. This was in 1849, the year Burbank was born, and it was in the very same town of Concord, twenty miles east of the Burbanks, where Thoreau and Emerson held forth. (Bull's neighbor was Bronson Alcott, Louisa May's father. It was Alcott who introduced him to the idea of selective breeding.) Bull named the grape after the town, and the reception for the Concord grape was overwhelming. He partnered with a company to sell the vines and made more than three thousand dollars in the first year they were on sale. But since he had no claim on the grape—there was no patent protection for fruit breeders—anyone who got his hands on it could not only grow as much as he wanted, but could also sell the vines to other interested growers. Sales tapered even as the Concord became the country's most popular grape. Bull grew disgusted with the fruit business and got out. Meanwhile, a man named Thomas Welch hit upon the idea of bottling juice from the Concord. By the time he made his fortune with what would evolve into Welch's grape juice, Bull was broke and living in an old folks' home. When he died, the epitaph on his grave read: HE SOWED, OTHERS REAPED.

Early in his career, when the subject of patenting plants came up, Burbank seemed to oppose the idea on the grounds that plants were "a law unto themselves." But after decades of endless crossing and recrossing had resulted in fame but no fortune, Burbank concluded that without any legal protection for the plant breeder, he "would hesitate to advise a young man, no matter how gifted or devoted, to adopt plant breeding as a life work." And so, before he died in 1926, he did endorse the idea of a law that would grant the breeder some protection. Several years later, when the United States Congress was considering just such a bill, Burbank's endorsement proved crucial. The bill had stalled in the House of Representatives, mostly due to the resistance of Congressman Fiorello La Guardia, of New York. In the course of debate, when he was asked by a congressman from Indiana what he thought of Burbank, La Guardia said, "I think he is one of the greatest Americans that ever lived." The congressman from Indiana responded by reading a letter that Burbank had written to Paul Stark, who was then the head of Stark Brothers Nursery. The letter read in part:

I have been for years in correspondence with leading breeders, nurserymen, and Federal officials and I despair of anything being done at present to secure to the plant breeder any adequate returns for his enormous outlays of energy and money . . . A man can patent a mouse trap or copyright a nasty song, but if he gives to the world a new fruit that will add millions to the value of earth's annual harvests he will be fortunate if he is rewarded by so much as having his name connected with the result.

La Guardia immediately reversed his position, and the Plant Patent Act of 1930 soon became law. It gave breeders seventeen years of protection against competition on varieties they hybridized or selected after open pollination. (Later, it would be extended to twenty years.) More to the point, the Act allowed breeders to profit from their work. Thomas Edison, who was awarded more than one thousand patents during his life, had also helped to push the measure through Congress. He insisted that by providing some financial incentives to breeders, the Plant Patent Act would "give us many Burbanks."

One of those many Burbanks was Fred Anderson. As a young man, Anderson apprenticed for Luther Burbank in Santa Rosa. Eventually, he moved to the San Joaquin Valley and settled in Le Grand, where he would do the work that would earn him the designation as the Father of the Modern Nectarine and where he would hire a young man named Floyd Zaiger to come work alongside him.

ONCE HE AND Betty decided to moonlight as fruit breeders, Floyd had to start building up a wide enough gene pool for his operation. A wider gene pool means more genetic diversity, more individual traits at your disposal as a breeder. Having a wide gene pool doesn't make you a great breeder, just as shopping at a huge supermarket doesn't make you a great cook. On the other hand, if you have access to only a limited number of ingredients, there's only so much you can do in the kitchen.

Floyd needed fruit trees and lots of them, so he called on his friend John Wynne, who was now running the Dave Wilson Nursery. Every year, the nursery had a big burn pile of seedlings and stock that they hadn't sold or used, and John offered Floyd a couple hundred of these trees. He wouldn't let Floyd pay him, but he said, "If you ever get something good, I want to be the first in line to introduce it." They shook on it and that was that.

There were several main challenges for Floyd and other breeders at this time. Most of the widely grown commercial peaches, plums, and nectarines were older varieties that ate well but were not ideally suited for the industrial food system that had sprung up after the Second World War. This was, after all, the golden age of food processing and the beginning of the rise of chain stores; consistency, durability, appearance, and a long shelf life were the emerging values for food. Also, most of the fresh stone fruit varieties were compressed into a short, summer growing season that started June 1 and ended at the very start of August. If fruit breeders could develop varieties that matured earlier or later, they could extend the season and help growers make more money.

Since most of the Zaigers' property was filled with azaleas, Floyd went around to nearby growers and offered to "rent" fruit trees from them for twenty dollars apiece. He hired three young women who had just moved from Mexico and he put them in charge of pollenizing the trees he'd rented. (Forty years later, one of the women, Flora, is still in charge of pollenizing, though her crew has grown to handle a considerably greater volume of trees.) Using those trees as the female parents, they pollenized them in February and then picked the fruit over the course of the summer. As they picked the fruit, they stripped off the flesh from the pit so that they could germinate the hybrid seed.

Still, they needed more space for all those seedlings, and so Floyd leased five acres from a neighbor. At night, when all the azalea business had been tended to and the kids had gone to sleep, he and Betty planted those seedlings by the light of the moon. The first year they had the five extra acres, they planted about eight hundred seedlings. But the next year, Floyd rented some other types of trees from different neighbors, and Flora and the girls hauled the ladders around and pollenized those trees. In the summer, they picked the fruit and stripped off the flesh, then planted those seedlings. The second year, there were more than eight hundred to plant.

In May of 1961, Floyd caught his first break when he discovered a bud sport—a genetic mutation—in his orchard. Instead of the regular Springtime peaches he was expecting, one tree had fruit that was a little different. It ripened a few days before the rest, and the fruit was generally larger than the Springtimes. The skin had a higher blush and the yellow flesh was relatively firm. All these differences made it a potentially more attractive peach. So after successfully grafting over the mutant and evaluating it for a few years, Zaiger named the new variety Royal Gold. He was awarded a patent on it in 1966, five years after he first discovered it.

A couple of years later, Floyd took a trip over to Europe to see how his yellow-fleshed peach was doing over there. During a tour of the stone fruit–growing areas of France, Floyd noticed that white-fleshed peaches and nectarines were often selling for twice what the yellow-fleshed fruit fetched. The whites had a few things going for them that the traditional varieties back home lacked. In general, they tended to have less acid, so their flavor was milder. Also, the whites tended to give off more of that peachy aroma. "I tell everybody that the French want to inhale half of their peach and eat the other half," Floyd said.

The big question mark with white-fleshed peaches and nectarines was their shipping quality. When ripe, they were very soft. In Europe, this wasn't such a big deal; growers there could fully ripen their fruit before they shipped it, because they weren't shipping very far. Shipping from France to Belgium was like us going from Modesto to Los Angeles. But if you tried to put ripe fruit from California on a truck to Boston, you'd have four or five days of bumping down the road, and the fruit would be mush by the time it got to the stores. Mostly for that reason, no California growers were interested in white-fleshed fruit and few American breeders had done any work on them. Remembering Fred Anderson's fig obsession, Floyd said, "Since no one had done much with them, I realized that everything I did would look good."

Back home, Floyd started working on building some firmness into white-fleshed peaches and nectarines. It was becoming more and more common in California to pick "green" fruit that was harder and could better withstand long-distance shipping, and the lower acid of the whites also meant that they tasted sweeter when they were picked before they were ripe. He was still concerned that the whites wouldn't be accepted in America, but they were popular in Asia, and many Californian growers had started shipping fruit to the Pacific Rim. The white-fleshed peaches and nectarines did go over well there, so well in fact that everybody wanted in on the action. Eventually, there were more than enough whites being grown in California to satisfy Asian demand. So the growers started shipping whites within the United States, and they found that, with a little marketing, American consumers were open to white-fleshed fruit, too. Today, roughly 30 percent of the peaches and nectarines sold in the United States have white flesh. Whether you love a low-acid, white-fleshed peach that crunches like an apple or rue the day that peaches stopped dripping down your chin as you ate them, you have the Zaigers to thank for it.

By the mid-1970s, Floyd had increased the volume of his gene pool enough to start focusing on pedigree. (Of all the descriptions I've heard about the art-science of fruit breeding, David Ramming's is the best. Ramming is the USDA's main plum and grape breeder in California. You have to have volume, Ramming said when I met him once. That was a necessary but insufficient condition. "But breeding is based on genetics, and genetics is a field of chance. I liken it to gambling. If you go to Las Vegas and play blackjack, and you don't know the game, what are your chances of winning? Not very good. If you know the cards—which cards are high, what the cards mean, what the chances are that certain cards will appear and in which combinations—and if you can remember what's been played, you increase your chances of winning, even though it's still a game of chance.")

In fruit breeding, if you know the inheritance scheme of the traits you want to improve (say you want to add size to an existing variety of plum) then you can plan the breeding methods (by crossing it with plums that have already been successful in passing along size). And if you can get better at identifying the traits you're looking for, and if you can pick them out earlier, then you're increasing your chances of winning. Anything you can do to improve your chances is important, and luck doesn't hurt either. (Gary Player is instructive here: The more you cross, the luckier you get.)

Hybrid trees that have more than one species in their genetic makeup are called "interspecific" trees. The Zaigers moved into interspecifics when they got into the development of rootstock, the hardy, disease-resistant base tree onto which commercial growers graft new varieties. A rootstock is not developed for its fruit; instead, it's like the engine on top of which a variety is built. The right rootstock can withstand less-than-ideal soil types and protect a tree from pests and diseases. Good rootstock can also help to make the fruit grow faster, bigger, and sweeter, and can produce a greater volume of fruit. In a patented cultivar the Zaigers called Citation, they had their first rootstock star. Citation is a peach-plum hybrid that is now a standard rootstock for growers of plums and apricots in California. Though the patent on Citation expired years ago, Floyd still keeps a couple of trees as ornamentals along a long wall of a storage barn next to the greenhouse where they do all of their crossing. On the last day of the spring visit I made to Zaiger Genetics, we stopped to look at Citation. The flowers were open and Floyd pulled one off. He held it up for me to see.

"These are like mules," he said, pointing into the flower. "There are anthers there but you see there's no pistil in it, so it can't set fruit. Why, for these rootstocks, we didn't care, because we propagated them from cuttings." Floyd dropped the flower, stepped back from the tree, looked at it with a smile on his face, and in the wistful tone a man might take when standing over the burial marker of a cherished hunting dog, said, "She was real good to us."

As we stood there next to Citation, Floyd explained the genealogy of another Zaiger rootstock called Viking, which is one-half peach, one-quarter almond, one-eighth plum, and one-eighth apricot. One year, Zaiger said, someone noticed two small fruits growing on a tree of *Prunus blireiana*, a plum tree with double pink flowers that's used as an ornamental. The fruits were fuzzy like an apricot, and the Zaigers figured they were straight plumcots, a cross made by the bees. They germinated the seeds and babied the seedlings, which were so genetically unstable that they almost refused to grow. Eventually, the Zaigers coaxed out some flowers. From the flowers, they took pollen and used it on an almond tree. Those crosses resulted in a couple of fruits, and the Zaigers germinated the pits to get seedlings.

"One of them grew that high"—he spread his index finger and thumb apart—"and then died. The other grew like a weed."

Grafting in a new variety of fruit is a big investment of time and money for a grower. The old variety gets chainsawed, leaving only the trunk of the rootstock onto which the new variety is then grafted. But if a new variety has more potential, then it's worth the investment of time and money. To put in new rootstock, though, is much more daunting: The old trees must be uprooted and burned, the soil fumigated, the new trees planted. It's a once-every-twenty-years undertaking. You don't just wake up one morning and decide to treat yourself to new rootstock.

Because of this, breeders tend to aim more precisely when developing rootstock. What quality is lacking in what you have? Which specific problem needs to be addressed? As the Zaigers continued to work on the rootstock that eventually would become Viking, they had two problems in mind. One was that almond trees tended to blow over in high winds. Another was that peaches tended to do poorly in high-alkaline soil. If you plant a plum in high-alkaline soil, its root hairs secrete acid and neutralize the soil, so that it can pick up iron and zinc and the other nutrients that turn the tree green. If you have a peach tree in that same soil, the tree's all yellow. It can't pick up that iron and zinc, because it doesn't secrete the acid to neutralize the soil.

The Zaigers now had an interspecific seedling that was one-quarter apricot, one-quarter plum, and one-half almond. Hoping to combine the plum's tolerance for alkaline soil with some base strength and disease resistance, Floyd used the pollen from the interspecific on a classic peach rootstock called Nemaguard. From that cross, the Zaigers grew thousands of seedlings until, after some years, they finally selected out Viking. It was compatible with both almonds and peaches. It helped produce a strong, large, and consistent set of fruit on the tree. It did relatively well in marginal soils. And when a strong wind came blowing through the orchard, its deep root system kept it firmly anchored to the ground.

The Viking story sounded like many other varietal histories, which always started with someone noticing something unfamiliar in a familiar setting. Something had been one way, and then it was another way. *I was walking through the orchard one day when I noticed a little fuzz on some plums.* In the neat narrative of Floyd's story, it sounded as if Viking had been planned all along, destined. As if all he had to do was show up. But at each step there was a new choice. Some people wouldn't have noticed the *blireiana* fruit. Some people wouldn't have bothered germinating the pits. Some people wouldn't have babied the seedlings, or used the pollen on an almond tree. Some people wouldn't have crossed the next hybrid with peach. It was like the stories couples tell about how they've ended up together. The telling makes it sound inevitable, but it's always anything but.

In the beginning, all of the interspecifics were sterile, like Citation and Viking. Many interspecifics had what's called a fasciated (or flat) pistil. Or they had no pistil and all pollen. Or they had no pollen. Whatever the condition, the flowers wouldn't set fruit. With plums and apricots, this is a notorious problem. (Writing about his plumcots in a book chapter entitled "Accomplishing the Impossible," Luther Burbank noted that one of his first plumcots "did not have a stamen on the whole tree.") But Floyd knew it *could* happen because Burbank had done it and because he'd seen that the bees could do it. Maybe on one out of every hundred thousand trees, he'd find an interspecific that was the doing of the bees. And so when he had enough volume of these interspecific seedlings, some of them did start fruiting, and that gave him avenues to take off down to see if he could create a new fruit.

Back in his office, Floyd knelt beside a small bookcase and pulled out a gigantic black binder from a row of gigantic black binders. Above the bookcase, I noticed a piece of computer paper tacked to the wood-paneled wall. In dot matrix Courier was a quote: "Having brilliant ideas is easy. Just have a lot of ideas and throw away most of them." It was attributed to Linus Pauling, the so-called Father of Molecular Biology (who won his first Nobel Prize, in chemistry, in 1954 as Zaiger was just starting out with azaleas). For a fruit breeder, those words are gospel. Having a lot of ideas won't guarantee a brilliant one, but the greater the diversity of desirable traits you have in your gene pool and the more crosses you make, the better the odds are that you'll come away with something worth keeping.

Floyd had found what he was looking for in the binder, which held years' worth of notes about the crosses they'd made. These particular notes were on plum–apricot crosses the Zaigers made in the late 1970s. Floyd ran his index finger down a column on the right side of the page. "Okay, look at this. 'Very poor growth.' 'Very poor growth.' 'No growth.'" He flipped a page. "'All died.' 'All died.' 'All died.' And that's down the whole page. This is that F1 sterility." Then, he turned an inch or two of pages to scan near the back of the binder. "But sooner or later, you found some that had good growth. Keep in mind this is years and years of going up and down the rows and finding almost all dead trees. But finally, you get to a year where you start to see"—his finger skipped down the page—"'Good growth.' 'Good growth.' 'Good growth.'" Once the Zaigers got enough of this good growth, they were able to keep crossing these first-generation plumcots back to a plum or an apricot. That's when they started to see a few with some interesting fruit.

To cross plums and apricots, the Zaigers at first mimicked a technique that Anderson and others had used. They built small wood-frame-and-wire houses around the plum trees they wanted to pollinate. When the blossoms were at that ideal popcorn stage, they placed branches from several different varieties of apricot inside the house along with a small hive of bees to do the pollinating. You could call it "controlled open pollination." Having different apricots in there meant that more genetic material was thrown into the mix, so it helped increase the Zaigers' chances of getting some viable seedlings. What they didn't consider at the time was the impossibility of getting a clean record of the resulting hybrids' genealogy. With bees pulling pollen from four or more different apricot branches, there was no way to know for sure which apricot's genes were being passed down to which plumcot. But a strict genealogical record of their selections was not what they were after. They were after new varieties of fruit.

Still, as the Zaigers' volume of fruit grew, the importance of record-keeping became apparent. Leith, who'd brought some paperwork into the office for Floyd to look over, picked up the conversation. "As we got a couple of generations out, we were looking at all these characteristics, studying them so that we'd have a better-educated guess about what from our gene pool we wanted to use to try to get certain results. There was just too much fruit. You couldn't keep track of everything." In 1977, the Zaigers started keeping records on every cross they made and any selections they took from those crosses. Each selection received an alphanumeric code noting where in the field the fruit was and from which generation it was crossed. The code corresponded to a written record that had the tree's lineage and statistics: its average Brix, its maturity time, its possible pollenizers, and so on. At first, everything was hand-written. Eventually, they moved to computers, but they still keep paper files on everything in card boxes and have a massive binder they've named "Andrew" that serves as their indexed black book.

After they had focused for so long on building up volume,

the record keeping allowed them to start working on pedigree. "Now we know how strong the inheritable characteristics are in our parents," Leith said. "We know which ones to draw on to try to get large size. We know which ones to use to try to get high color. We know which ones to use for low chilling. Well, wait—let me rephrase that: We always *think* we know which ones will carry large size, higher color, low chilling requirements. We've been studying all these characteristics for years, but it is still a numbers game, you know. You've still got to throw the dice and see which way you come up. But we just hope we've put the odds a little more in our favor."

Out in the field, the Zaigers made two other important improvements: They built a large, tented greenhouse for making crosses, and they borrowed a trick from their ornamental nursery business and started planting fruit trees in container tubs. (I remembered seeing that forest of blue tubbed trees for the first time and hearing Leith say, *Those are the female parents for our crosses.*) With the mother trees in containers, the Zaigers could easily move them around and take the trees to the pollen instead of taking the pollen out to the trees. To pollinate a tree, they moved it into the greenhouse, where, over the course of several days, all the tree's flowers would be dabbed with pollen. (Previously, they'd had to retrace their steps, hopscotching all over the orchard to make the crosses.) This way, they were able to make a wider range of crosses in less time. They also found that the ideal temperature for making a cross—the most fertile temperature for pollen tube growth—is 60 degrees Fahrenheit. Out in the field, it might get too hot or too cold. But inside the greenhouse, they could set the mood and keep the air at that ideal temperature. Plus, out of the fog and the cold and the rain, the greenhouse was just a nicer place to work.

By the late 1980s, the Zaigers' fruit breeding was starting to pay for itself. Over thirty years, the family had expanded its ornamental nursery business to include several retail outlets, plus wholesale and landscaping divisions. But the success of the white-fleshed peaches and nectarines and the interspecific rootstock had turned the fruit breeding into more than just a hobby. In 1989, the Zaigers sold the ornamental nursery business, just as their work with interspecific fruits was starting to show results.

Here's what happened in the first several years after the Zaigers sold their plant nursery to focus on stone fruit: The California plum market tanked, and then the industry self-destructed.

At the root of the problem was the fact that many of the plums being packed were not particularly great, at least not compared to the older generation of smaller, more delicate plums—the Burmosas, the Santa Rosas, the El Dorados. For years, growers and packers had reported that retailers wanted fruit that was "big, red, and hard," and so that's what breeders in California had been working on. (What had made the Zaigers' Royal Gold peach worth patenting? *The fruit was generally larger than the Springtimes. The skin had a higher blush and the yellow flesh was relatively firm.*) And when breeders came out with an improvement—something bigger, something with more color, something harder—it not only helped growers deliver what the retailers wanted in the short term (arguably good), but it also validated the retailers' expectations that fruit could and should be big, red, and hard (inarguably bad). A produce buyer might see a new, big red rock of a variety and say to growers, "Bring me more like this." The growers would then go back to the breeders, and the breeders would try to produce a solution. By the 1980s, this cycle had all but washed out the importance of flavor. With flavor so low on the list of priorities as to be negligible and with growers picking the fruit earlier and earlier to give it a longer shelf life, plenty of the plum varieties looked good in the produce section, but when you ate them, you didn't necessarily feel like you'd gotten a good return on your investment. They were not plums that inspired repeat sales. They were farmer-friendly and retail-friendly, but they were not consumer-friendly. In terms of eating quality, plums had devolved. That was problem number one.

The second major problem was that there were way too many plums being shipped out of California in the late 1980s. This was due in part to the messy decentralization of the industry that David Albertson had described to me, the dissolution of the so-called Big Eight. As commercial packers, the Big Eight contracted with individual growers for the course of the season. When there were hundreds of buyers on the retail end but the bulk of the sales were going through the Big Eight, it was still a seller's market, and the industry could afford to think in terms of volume.

But in the mid-1980s, the retail game was changing. Buyers were moving away from volume and starting to pay more for larger fruit. While all varieties have certain genetic limitations on how large they can get, the grower can do a lot to affect fruit size: how much and when he waters, how much and how carefully he thins his trees, which nutrients he uses on his trees, how long he lets the fruit stay on the tree. Growing larger fruit often meant growing less of it per tree. But if it cost the same amount—say, four dollars per box—to grow, pick, and pack large plums as it did to grow, pick, and pack small plums, and if buyers were paying twelve dollars per box for large plums and six dollars per box for small plums, then the advantage was obvious.

This transition from volume to size was one factor that was breaking up the hegemony of the Big Eight and creating a great flourishing of smaller, independent packing sheds who wanted more control over when and how they packed their fruit. Those who saw what was happening on the retail side and reacted accordingly were able to do fairly well during this time. But in the late 1980s, much of the industry was still growing for volume, and so record plum crops were coming out of California. Most of those plums were small. The result was that a lot of growers were losing money.

On top of that, the California plum industry itself was falling apart. There were complaints among growers and packers that the standards for quality and size were being enforced arbitrarily. Certain packers were hovered over and inspected almost box-by-box while other packers were allowed to ship whatever they wanted. Not only were some growers fed up with the way inspections were being carried out, a group of them was frustrated with the idea of inspections altogether. They channeled this frustration toward the California Tree Fruit Agreement. The CTFA had been created during the New Deal as part of the "federal marketing order" movement. Marketing orders are strange hybrid things—trade associations that act a little like miniature, semiprivate governments. They were created to give farmers of certain crops the power to set standards for and collectively promote the crops they grew. When a federal marketing order for a certain crop was created in a certain area, anyone who grew that crop in that area was automatically included in the marketing order. Participation, much to the displeasure of many an independent-minded farmer, was usually mandatory.

In 1933, three marketing orders were enacted for the California peach, plum, and nectarine growers, and the CTFA was created as an umbrella organization to manage them. Each crop has its own central committee within the CTFA, and there are also subcommittees that oversee research budgets and quality standards. But the main function of the CTFA has always been to promote California's plums, peaches, and nectarines to consumers, and the money for that generic promotion comes from the growers themselves; for every box of fruit shipped, growers must pay what's called an assessment fee. Each arm of the CTFA sets its own assessment fee—usually in the ballpark of twenty cents per box—and then revisits the amount every several years when it holds a referendum on whether or not to continue with the marketing order.

The CTFA was an easy target: With the glut of lackluster plums, the shift from volume to size, the market in the gutter, and the widespread belief that inspections were done unfairly, dissatisfaction with the marketing order was at an all-time high. In the late 1980s, a small group of growers began withholding their assessment fees from the CTFA to protest against the size standards. Eventually, the group sued the USDA, arguing both that the standards for peaches, plums, and nectarines were "arbitrary and capricious" and that their being forced to participate in the federal plum marketing order's generic promotion was a violation of their free speech. Why, these growers argued, should they be forced to pay for generic promotion of all plums—promotion that essentially put forth the idea that all plums were equally good—when the goal of their in-house promotion was to convince customers that their plums were better than everybody else's? Weren't they being forced to compete against themselves? For an interesting glimpse into what a Court of Appeals judge called "one of the more byzantine, and all-encompassing, areas of federal regulation," read the summary of *Wileman Brothers and Elliott vs. Espy*. (Michael Espy was the U.S. Secretary of Agriculture at the time.) The same judge wrote in his opinion: "The complexity of the legal proceedings in this case have been matched by their prolixity." Eventually, a variant of the case made it to the United States Supreme Court, which ruled five to four against the growers.

There had been lawsuits against other marketing orders in the past (the mushroom case was a doozy), but this was a defining moment for California stone fruit growers, who had, for the most part, always operated according to the principle that the rising tide lifts all boats. With the Wileman lawsuit out in the open and the growing realization among growers that the quality of what you packed was becoming as much a factor as the quantity, there was a prevailing sense that when the tide took you out, no one else would be there to make sure that you had battened down your own hatches.

And so, in the early 1990s, when plum growers were presented with the usually routine vote on whether to continue participating in the federal marketing order, they acted on their dissatisfaction and voted themselves out of the CTFA and into a voluntary growers' association. In so doing, they freed themselves up from minimum-size standards and the per-box assessment fee. Freedom, at least, was the idea. But the secession was a flop. Without a central command, the plum industry lacked the ability to report even to itself the nature and volume of its pack-outs. Plum growers saw an immediate decline in both the overall volume of the crop and the average price per box they got from retailers. So a couple of years later, in 1994, the plum growers repented and returned to the CTFA. This time, instead of resuscitating the federal marketing order that had been in place before the break, they set up a state marketing order that looked, smelled, and felt much like the initial arrangement, only this time they worked with oversight from the California Department of Food and Agriculture (CDFA) instead of the USDA.

Soon after the creation of the state marketing order, another plum grower filed another complaint, this time against the CDFA, citing a similar restriction on free speech, but according to the California constitution, not the U.S. one. The case made it to the Supreme Court of California, which sided with the grower and remanded the case back to the lower court, which had based its earlier decision on the Wileman ruling by the U.S. Supreme Court. That case, which was eventually settled out of court, was filed by a family of stone fruit growers named Gerawan.

All this drama fostered a general sense among many California stone fruit growers that plums were no longer worth the trouble. A joke that still circulates summed up the ill will. "A peach is like your mother: It's always there for you. A nectarine is like your girlfriend: It's something really dear and special. A plum is like the harlot down the street: It'll screw you every time." Growers were sick of being screwed by plums. They were a headache. *Plum* was a dirty word.

So it was not the best time for the Zaigers to begin introducing a line of plum hybrids. But that's exactly what they did.

One of their first introductions was variety 35EA376, a fifty-fifty plumcot they patented as Flavorella. They'd selected it from an open-pollinated cross of an unknown apricot and a plum called Red Beaut, which Fred Anderson had patented in the mid-1960s. (Anderson had selected Red Beaut from a cross he'd made between an old variety called El Dorado and another called Burmosa, which at that time was one of the earliest-ripening plums in California. When Red Beaut was released in 1965, El Dorado and Burmosa made up nearly 15 percent of the California plum crop. Ten years later, there were as many Red Beauts shipped out of California as there were El Dorados and Burmosas combined. By 1988, Red Beaut was one of the most widely grown plums in the state, while El Dorado and Burmosa were pretty much relics.) Flavorella has, in the language of plant patents, "scant down," meaning a soft, short apricot-like fuzz that's almost undetectable. Depending on the year, Flavorella's skin is greenish-yellow to rich, butternut orange. It's on the smaller side and it's juicy but not dripping, its flesh more apricot than plum. It's not an outstanding piece of fruit by today's standards—the average Brix listed in the patent was only 14.6—but when ripe the smell will make you loopy.

It is common for growers to test new varieties for breeders. In exchange for providing information to the breeder about how the variety performs, the grower gets a small number of trees to plant in his orchard. The breeder gets a sense of how the variety will perform in certain climates and soil conditions, while the grower will have a jump on the variety if it looks like a winner. After some testing of Flavorella, growers reported one major problem with the variety: To get any flavor out of the fruit, you had to wait until it was ripe; but if you let it sit on the tree even one day too long, it dropped. A lot of people loved the novelty of Flavorella, but the picking of it was almost prohibitive. One grower who tested it told Floyd that he would lie awake at night and just hear it go plop, plop, plop. Some growers went to the extreme of spreading a straw-covered canvas net under the trees to soften the fall. But that wasn't something you could do for quantity on a commercial scale.

Because of the drop problem, Flavorella fizzled. But the Zaigers were just getting started with the interspecifics. In the late 1980s, they patented three plum-apricot hybrids that were at least a generation beyond Flavorella. The Zaigers had selected two of the varieties from backcrosses they made between a first-generation plumcot and a plum. As with Flavorella, the plumcot in both cases was a selection taken from an open-pollinated Red Beaut seedling. (The plum they used for the backcross was Mariposa, an older variety that was known in some circles as

"Improved Satsuma" because it was thought to be the open-pollinated offspring of Burbank's original "Blood Plum.") The Zaigers named these first two varieties Flavor Supreme and Flavor Queen, and they averaged 17 and 18 Brix, respectively. The third variety also averaged 18 Brix. It was called Flavor King. It was the result of one plum-apricot hybrid being crossed with another plum-apricot hybrid—plumcot X plumcot. (A decade later at Chez Panisse, it was Flavor King that would be served alone as the finale of a sixty-five-dollar prix fixe menu.)

The Zaigers had patented the three varieties because the Dave Wilson Nursery wanted to sell them in its new home garden division. But in order to sell them, they needed a name. Even though the hybrids were mostly plum, they couldn't really call them "plums" because the varieties had apricot genes in their family trees. But they couldn't call them "plumcots" either, because for decades that name had been used only for first-generation plum-apricot crosses like Flavorella. Locked out of the existing taxonomy, the Zaigers decided to trademark their own name. In their 1989 application with the United States Patent and Trademark Office, they dropped the two middle consonants of the word that was closest to what they had and just decided to call the things "pluots."

The grower who had lain awake at night listening to Flavorella drop was Mike Jackson. The oldest son of David Jackson's older brother George, and one of the heads of the Kingsburg Orchards empire, Mike was undeterred by his experience. He wanted to try these pluots. Never mind that they were meant for the home garden market, and not commercial growers.

Never mind that Flavor Supreme looked like a warped and dulled six ball or that Flavor King had a bad problem with cracking. The Jacksons had decided to "chase flavor." Before they worried about a variety being farmer-friendly, they wanted it to taste good. That was their niche, and pluots fit in it nicely.

Around the time of the plum industry's self-destruction, Mike bought a ranch from a local grower named Wayne Adams. Like the Jacksons, Adams had been testing some of the Zaigers' varieties. One of the unpatented pluots that Adams had been testing was a light red fruit mottled with gray-green streaks and dotted with pale sugar spots. It was big for a plum and heavy for its size, squat and round-cheeked. Just inside the skin, the flesh had a filament of bright red, fading to a pinkish-white. The fruit's average 17.4 Brix was a lot of sugar for that time, and it hit the mouth as a flat, candy-simple sweet—not complex but not at all tart.

Mike hadn't seen this numbered variety before, but after spending a little time with it, he liked what he saw. It appeared to set well and had as its pollenizer Flavor Queen, the sweet, yellowish pluot the Jacksons were already testing. The variety had few cosmetic problems—aside from its inherent mottledness—and seemed to hold up well to shipping. Adams had been one of the first to test the variety, and it still hadn't been seen by that many growers, many of whom had plum-fatigue anyway. Seeing an opportunity, the Jacksons placed a big order with the Dave Wilson Nursery.

In their patent application, the Zaigers called the variety Dapple Dandy. They wrote that it was "a cross between a plum selection with the identification No. 58GA338 and a plumcot selection of unknown parentage. The plum selection with the identification No. 58GA338 originated from a cross between Laroda Plum (non-patented) and Queen Ann Plum (non-patented). A large group of seedlings were planted and grown under careful observation by us and one such seedling which represents the present variety, being especially desirable for its fruit quality was selected for asexual reproduction and commercialization."

Wayne Adams had mentioned that Dapple Dandy kind of looked like a "dinosaur egg." (*Jurassic Park* had recently become the most successful movie of all time.) The Jacksons thought so, too, and they trademarked the name. When they had their first sizable harvest in the mid-1990s, they picked the fruit as ripe as possible and sent Dapple Dandy to grocery stores with a special label: On each piece of fruit they placed an oval sticker with a picture of a smiling apatosaurus and the name "Dinosaur Egg." The sweet, mottled fruit was a hit.

After Dinosaur Egg had been out in the market for a couple of years, what was amazing to those paying attention was that many of the retailers who did business with the Jacksons were actually carving out a separate space for the fruit. Long accustomed to retailers lumping all plums into the "black" bin and the "red" bin, they were even more amazed when the stores started using the Jacksons' brand name on in-store signs. The stores were selling Dinosaur Eggs—not plums, not pluots, not Dapple Dandies. Most amazing of all was that by the late 1990s, when many plum varieties were spoiling in the store at a dollar or so a pound, Dinosaur Eggs were regularly selling out at nearly four times the price.

The success did not go unnoticed. In July 1998, *Good Fruit Grower* magazine ran an article entitled "New Fruit Hybrids Are Moving into Mainstream." In it, Robert Woolley, the head of the Dave Wilson Nursery, estimated that more than two thousand acres of pluots had been planted since 1994. "It's astonishing how it's taking off," Woolley was quoted in the article. "I've been told that we're at a point where the nectarine industry was forty years ago."

Pluots had arrived.

6

IN EARLY APRIL 2007, the CTFA sent out a press release called "PPN: A Great Start." It read:

The California peach, plum, and nectarine industry is expecting an excellent 2007 crop.

"We've had a great start to the growing season," said CTFA President Sheri Mierau. "Favorable winter and spring weather have created ideal conditions for peach, plum, and nectarine development to this point."

A cool winter delivered more than 1,000 chilling hours, meaning peach, plum, and nectarine trees were well rested coming into the spring bloom season. The ample chill hours resulted in a strong, uniform bloom, which led into a beautiful warm, dry spring. The warm, dry spring weather is conducive to the development of fruit with high sugars and a great-tasting eating experience.

The warm, dry spring of 2007 resembles that of the spring of 2004, a year that delivered what was widely agreed to be the best-tasting California peach, plum, and nectarine crop in ten years. The industry believes it is on track for comparable fruit quality this season . . .

A superstitious grower might have been troubled by the comparison to 2004. That year did deliver "what was widely agreed to be the best-tasting California peach, plum, and nectarine crop in ten years," but it was also the year that was widely agreed to have been, as Ballantine's Rick Milton had put it, a "bloodbath."

But then, around Easter, something auspicious happened: One of the worst freezes on record hit the southeastern United States. All the southern trees were fruiting by that time, and most of the crop was lost. It was devastating for southern growers but it did bode well for the guys in California who wouldn't have to compete with the South's fruit—notably its peaches—during the first part of the season. This was important not just because box prices were often high at the beginning of the season, but also because those weeks before Memorial Day were crucial in setting the tone for the rest of the summer. If California growers could deliver great-tasting fruit right from the get-go, then supermarkets might see early repeat sales and the marketers could ride the momentum and start moving a lot of fruit.

When I checked in with Rod Milton, he was optimistically cautious. His major concern—of the ones he knew about—was the size of the fruit. Because of the strong bloom and the warm, dry spring, the early varieties were maturing faster than normal and might not have enough time for the fruit to develop to the right size up and down the tree. Size was usually something the stores wouldn't budge on, but if the early fruit was eating well, he could live with it being a little small, especially since California growers wouldn't be competing with fruit from the South.

What really gnawed at Rod were the unknowables.

"Seasons always surprise you," he said. "By this point, there's a certain amount of predictability, but every season there's always something that surprises you."

By mid-May, however, when Rod began picking pluots, the outlook was still good. While the first fruit that came off the tree felt closer in size to a racquetball than a cue ball, its flavor was off the charts. The initial reports from Ballantine seemed promising. Fruit was moving out the door.

It was moving, too, at Family Tree Farms, and across the street the golf course at Ridge Creek was taking shape as machines smoothed over mounds of dirt—future fairways—and a bridge in the foreground connected two roads that looped away from the main road and out of sight.

David Jackson's sales team was prioritizing "program sales" that hadn't yet kicked in. "Program sales" described a relatively new way of thinking about fruit sales that was more in line with how supermarkets were now doing business. In the days before mass consolidation on the retail side, when there had been a great sea of potential buyers, selling fruit had been all about the spot market, selling that particular day's fruit. Salesmen would get to the office at four or five o'clock in the morning and stay until six or seven at night. They were always working the phones, making sales, thriving on the juice. It was intense and exhilarating, and the job had a high burnout rate.

Today, with so few buyers and with the volume game fading, that way of business just didn't make sense anymore for operations like Family Tree. Buyers were looking for a consistent, steady supply of fruit, and so Family Tree and other sales companies tried to make it as easy as possible on buyers to get that fruit from one place. Setting up programs meant that Family Tree looked at what and how much fruit they planned to have over the coming season and when they planned to have it, and then they methodically tried to attach a buyer beforehand to as much of the fruit as possible.

Program sales usually didn't start until after Memorial Day. The hope was that the early-season stuff would move briskly enough so that the program sales could kick in at the beginning and run the course of the season. Of course, working the fruit into a program didn't guarantee that it would sell. Buyers were always looking around for deals, and stone fruit was, as several people noted, a "sell it or smell it" commodity. If a buyer was lagging and you had fruit stacking up in cold storage, you couldn't make the sale happen by hoping for it. Being able to get a good read on a buyer was still an old-school skill worth having. You had to know when to let go of the fruit while it was still worth something to somebody.

7

As the season got under way, the stone fruit consolidation that Ballantine's David Albertson had talked about over Armenian-Cajun food began to take shape behind the scenes. A former head of the CTFA named Blair Richardson announced that he was heading up a company called FreshSense, a federation of the sales and marketing divisions of half a dozen major packer-shippers, including Ballantine.

The companies involved in FreshSense accounted for about one third of all the stone fruit shipped out of California. They had already been working together in a loosely bound cooperative called Ripe 'n Ready which was based on the post-harvest "conditioning" program that called for cooling the fruit when it came in from the hot orchard. The goal of the Ripe 'n Ready alliance was to share knowledge and cooperate on a common business strategy. The alliance was too loose, though. None of the partners wanted to be the first to make a commitment, and so few commitments were made. FreshSense was the group's second try, and this time they vowed to work together, though they were still working out the logistics of the new organization, which wouldn't be active as a sales company until 2008 at best. The idea, though, was to consolidate the sales and marketing efforts of the different companies under one roof. If they could successfully control the box price for all the fruit they produced, then they could stabilize a much greater share of the industry.

The point of FreshSense, however, wasn't just to stabilize the price, Blair said one morning when we met for breakfast at the Blossom Trail Cafe, in Sanger. He was wearing a pressed blue button-down and drinking tea. The company also wanted to reach into the supply chain and be more involved with the fruit at the store level. "There's not a farmer out there who's going to rely on someone to harvest his fruit for him. So what are we doing letting someone have full control over the marketing of that fruit?" He mentioned the consumer packaged goods companies, which had some say in where and how their product was marketed in the store. Fruit growers put the fruit in a box at the packing house, loaded it onto a truck, and then it was gone.

"We have to become better partners for the retailers and start combining our resources," Blair said. The alternative was bleak. "We aren't all going to be able to survive individually," he continued. "There was the mass consolidation at the retail level in the mid-nineteen-nineties, and there hasn't been a strong enough reaction in the industry to confront that. You have to have an opposite and equal reaction to survive."

Blair was spending his first months on the job negotiating with the FreshSense packers, trying to figure out exactly how the company would be structured. The members had been each other's competitors for a long time, and, having failed to come together in any meaningful way in the Ripe 'n Ready deal, they were now talking about the best way to exist as partners. As Albertson said when I asked him about the group, they "were trying to figure out *how* to agree to *what* they had all agreed to. We don't want to be all black and white. We want to be all gray. But your gray may be light gray, and my gray may be dark gray. They're all gray but they're not the same gray."

It was Blair's job right now to get them all seeing the same shade of gray. It was not going to be easy, but his recent experience at the CTFA had been instructive. Blair had come to the CTFA with no experience in stone fruit. After attending Texas A&M on an ag scholarship, he had worked for a decade at a cotton cooperative based in Bakersfield. In the late 1990s, he and his family had moved to Sacramento, and he had commuted into San Francisco to work at a startup involved in online ag commodities trading. When the CTFA's long-time president had retired in 2001, the search committee had looked high and low for a replacement.

"Despite the fact, or maybe because of the fact, that I had no industry experience, they thought I might be right for the job," Blair said.

When he was hired at the CTFA in 2002, there were four outstanding grower lawsuits against the CTFA's Plum Marketing Board. (Three of those were settled during his tenure.) Maybe even more insidious than the direct animosity toward the CTFA was the industry's overwhelming indifference toward it. This was evident after the peach and nectarine referendum that took place during Blair's first months on the job. In the vote to decide whether they would continue participating in the marketing order, just over 10 percent of peach and nectarine growers even bothered to cast a vote.

Blair had undergone several rounds of interviews with CTFA members and staff, so he was aware of all these issues when he accepted the job. There was one big issue that he was not aware of, though, and it could be summed up in a word. The reason he was not aware of it was because no one had uttered that word during any of his interviews. And since he didn't even know the word existed, he couldn't have been expected to ask about it. The word was "pluot."

At first, pluots had seemed like an unambiguous blessing. With the reputation of plums at rock bottom, the California stone fruit industry now had a plum-like fruit that it could market as something new and different—or, at the very least, as something *else*. Not only could sales companies avoid the association with plums and work on negotiating a higher box price, they could also start to carve out more shelf space in the store for California stone fruit. In the mid-1990s, globalism was opening up American grocery stores to all kinds of new fresh produce. Claiming more real estate in the produce section was good for everybody in stone fruit.

There was one big problem, though, and the Dave Wilson Nursery's Robert Woolley found out about it after the nursery applied for a PLU for the pluot. If growers and marketers were going to ask retailers to pay more for pluots, then retailers would have to have the means to charge more for them in the store. To do that, they needed a separate code.

PLU codes are managed by a trade organization called the Produce Marketing Association (PMA). When an application for a new PLU comes in to the PMA, it has to have three letters of support from retailers. Two committees review the application and, assuming everything checks out, move it up to another committee called the Produce Electronic Identification Board, which consists of growers, shippers, retailers, and distributors. The PEIB votes to approve, deny, or request more information for an application. The pluot application never made it to the PEIB, because "pluot" is a privately held trademark, and privately held trademarks are not eligible for PLU codes. Certain regional trademarks have received PLU codes—for example, Vidalia onions (#4159), Walla Walla onions (#4163), and Maui onions (#4164). But since the trademark for "pluot" is owned by the Zaigers, it's comparable to something like the Ugli Fruit, a privately owned trademarked tangerine–pomelo hybrid which is known on its PLU sticker as the "Jamaican Tangelo" (#4459). Woolley scrambled to come up with another name. After consulting with growers, he submitted an application for "interspecific plum," which would cover any fruit that was a cross between two or more different plum species. The application was approved and pluots had their PLU code: #3278. As long as that number and the words "interspecific plum" (or "I.S. plum") were on the label somewhere, packers could brand the fruit however they wanted—Dinosaur Egg, Flavor Safari, whatever. The one thing they couldn't call a pluot was a "plum," but since the whole point was to distinguish pluots from plums, this suited the Jacksons and other early pluot growers just fine.

But as more and more growers planted pluots, the troubles started. Many retailers weren't interested in making space for yet another new fruit (especially one that seemed so similar—at least on the surface—to an existing fruit). There were issues too with sending pluots overseas, where the labeling nuances were lost in translation. Because of these problems, some packers ignored #3278 and started slapping plum labels on pluots instead. The shipment of plums is governed by the CTFA (which is bound by state law to maintain the integrity of the "plum" as a commodity), so the only way to allow pluots to be shipped as plums was to get the state of California to acknowledge that pluots were plums. Had everyone in the industry agreed that getting the state to recognize pluots as plums was a good idea, then the problem would have been solved. But not every grower did agree that this was a good idea. If the point was to carve out more space for this new fruit in the produce section and to brand it as something far superior to the old, humdrum plums, then allowing its brand to be diminished by an association with the old, humdrum plums was in fact a very bad idea, the exact opposite of what the industry needed to do.

There was another compelling reason not to call pluots plums, and it had to do with money. Because pluots were "interspecific plums" and "interspecific plums" were not included in the plum marketing order governed by the CTFA, then growers didn't have to pay an assessment fee on interspecific plums like they did on plums. The assessment fee was only twenty cents or so a box, but pluot acreage was increasing every year, and everyone could do the math.

Sides began forming in the industry, none of them especially clear-cut. Some growers took the strict line that since pluots supposedly had apricot in them, they could not be considered plums. Others argued that if pluots looked like plums, tasted like plums, could be sprayed like plums, and had retailers who wanted to call them plums, then they should just be called plums: the "If it walks like a duck . . ." argument. Some pointed out that since other "interspecific plums"—Burbank's Santa Rosa, for example, which was a hybrid of several different plum species—were included in the plum marketing order, then no exception could be made for pluots, especially since so many of them had so little apricot in them. Others insisted that it didn't really matter what pluots' genetic makeup was or what they walked like. The only thing that mattered was carving out the new niche in the marketplace. Still others were just constitutionally opposed to the CTFA and didn't want to see a new variety sucked into the marketing order.

Soon, the name-calling started. Those in favor of calling them pluots were "just trying to avoid paying assessment fees." Those who wanted to bring them into the marketing order and call them plums were "just trying to cash in on something that others had taken the risk on and established on their own." There were threats of lawsuits. One grower played chicken with the CTFA by suggesting that if he was forced to call his pluots plums, he would sue the Zaigers and Dave Wilson on the premise that he had thought he'd been buying plum-apricot hybrids. In an open letter, another grower vowed to ship his pluots as plums. If state inspectors tried to stop him, he threatened to sue the California Department of Food and Agriculture to force it to prove that his pluots were in fact not plums.

The CTFA assembled the first Plumcot Task Force in January 1998. By April, it was the Inter Specific Stone Fruit Task Force. By July, it was the InterSpecific Plum Task Force. Later that year, there was a hearing on pluots at the California Department of Food and Agriculture. After listening to all sides, the state decided to remain undecided about what to do with pluots. Until the industry itself could come to some consensus about what pluots were, the state would stay out of it.

Over the next few years, the tension over pluots continued to rise until finally, in 2001, Blair Richardson was brought in to clean up the mess. Over the winter of 2002–2003, the group by then known as the Interspecific Task Force met several times and finally came to what was probably going to be as much of a consensus as it would ever come to. Growers and packers could continue marketing pluots as "pluots" and labeling them as "interspecific plums," in which case they were on their own. They had no obligations to the CTFA for that fruit. (In fact, legally speaking, the CTFA could have nothing to do with that fruit.) Or, if a grower was willing to adhere to the CTFA's plum standards and pay the assessment fee, he could sell his pluots as "plums." In other words, pluots were whatever you needed them to be to make the sale.

There were still plenty of questions. Retailers reported that consumers were confused by the pluot vs. plum issue, and many buyers themselves weren't really sure what was going on. One store would buy pluots as "pluots" or "interspecific plums" while another store would buy pluots as "plums," and that just depended on different marketing strategies. The result was that you could go to two nearby stores and find the same variety sold as both a pluot and a plum, often for wildly different prices. Some of the intensity had been taken out of the issue within the industry. But out there in the supermarkets of summer, it was all muddled.

SUMMER

1

SATURDAY MORNING IN late July 2007. I was driving at dawn, stone fruit rush hour, in heavy traffic toward the Milton place in Parlier. The mountains ahead were in perfect resolution against the sky, their tops ringed in a yellow glow.

For a few weeks, I'd been hearing the same thing from every grower I talked to: After a promising start, peaches, plums, and nectarines were all in the tank. What baffled everyone was that even in years when the fruit quality left something to be desired, at least one of the three fruits tended to sell well if the other two were down. This season, though, peaches, plums, and nectarines tasted better than they had in years—even better than in 2004—but the average box price for all three crept lower and lower. And it was worse than just a low box price. Even with the volume of fruit down and the eating quality excellent across the board, the stores weren't running many sales, and fruit was stacking up in cold storage. Even with an industrywide fire sale in effect, salesmen were having trouble moving the fruit. Not only was the catch-as-catch-can spot market down, but the program sales were hurting, too. Stores were buying less fruit and they were paying less for it. It was a bloodbath in the making.

Speculation about the cause of the slump covered all the bases. The spring weather had been good to all kinds of fruit—berries, melons, grapes—so there was a lot for buyers to choose from. Fuel prices were so high that both stores and consumers were cutting back on everything but necessities. Several big chains were in the middle of union negotiations, and every time a package of fruit came into the distribution center, it had to be divided for multiple stores and then rewrapped for shipment to the store level. The more fruit they ordered, the more they spent on labor. And then there was the most depressing reason people in the industry could think of: Maybe all those Summer Passionates didn't like stone fruit as much as the marketers thought they did. Maybe people were just sick of plums.

Rod Milton's truck wasn't in the driveway at the house, so I dropped by and found him at the old packing shed next to his parents' place. When he saw me pull in, he waved his panama hat, hopped up on a tractor, and pointed at his truck. "Just follow me," he shouted. "I'm going down the avenue."

I left the car at the shed and, in Rod's truck, followed him down a narrow dirt road that led away from the street through the orchard. Behind the tractor, he was hauling white bins. We made a couple of turns and then Rod motioned for me to park the truck. He turned the tractor and disappeared between two rows of plum trees. I parked, got out, and wandered by myself in the opposite direction.

If you have no stake in it, there is no better place to be than an empty stone fruit orchard at dawn. The orderly trees stand close enough to form a cloister, but they're not so tall and dense as to crowd you. They have an indelible quality to them, while the sagging fruit reminds you that time is running out. A muffled quiet, as if someone has turned down the volume on the world, makes the orchard seem more like a setting than a place—a courtyard fountain, rather than a waterfall in the woods.

But then when you see an orchard worked, you get just enough of a peek into the mechanics of it to put the reverie to bed. When I heard Rod kill the tractor's engine behind me, I turned and walked back to find him. A crew of Latinos was working the trees, and I heard them whistling back and forth to each other, like a family of birds warning one another about a cat on the prowl. The pickers wore harnessed bags on their chests. Up in the tripod ladders that were a fixture in the Valley, they picked from the top down, working with both hands. The men were already soaked with sweat. There were murmurs in Spanish. When a picker's bag was full, he climbed down, un-hooked the flap at the bottom of the harness, and dumped the plums into one of the white bins behind the tractor. This bin packing was the standard in the industry and you could see why the fruit had to be picked at least a little green. Fully ripe fruit would be crushed.

Rod tossed me a plum—a Grand Rosa. "These are probably the last trees of it in the Valley." Grand Rosa was an old Fred Anderson variety. He patented it a year or so after Floyd Zaiger had left to start his own operation. Anderson had planted a row of El Dorado plums, which were self-incompatible, next to a row of Santa Rosas (which, incidentally, were self-compatible).

He'd taken open-pollinated seeds from the El Dorados and selected out seedlings that showed promise. One of them had become Grand Rosa. It was a nice-looking piece of fruit, purplish with yellow flesh, and even though it was a little crunchy for my taste, it was still a fine plum.

Rod was talking with a foreman about the schedule, which was continually re-calibrated through the thick of the season depending on what was happening with the fruit. If two varieties were coming off at the same time, or if one unexpectedly needed a few more days, then Rod had to shift around manpower. When he'd packed his own stuff, Rod had made all these decisions himself. Now that he was with Ballantine, he had to work with the packer on his picking schedule, and he occasionally grew frustrated by the back-and-forth that had to happen before stuff could get done. Today, this crew was going to finish out his Grand Rosas and then move over to his brother Rick's orchard in the afternoon, where there was a lot of work to be done on a plot of nectarines. Rod and his foreman went over the schedule one more time and agreed to touch base in a little bit if anything changed. As we got back in the truck and drove toward town for breakfast, he shook his head, frustrated, and said, "I'm just not used to doing so much talking."

He was frustrated as well by the way the season was turning out. The down market was *the* topic every Saturday morning when Rod met a crew of fruit people at a diner close to central Parlier. It was more kaffeeklatsch than breakfast. We were a little late, and when we arrived, half a dozen guys were already there, filling a couple of adjacent booths. Rod introduced me around and told the men that I was interested in the stone fruit business.

"Stone fruit welfare is more like it," said one guy, who introduced himself as an independent pest control adviser.

I asked them how many pluots they thought were out there in the market. One of them guessed that there were a quarter as many as there were plums. (Two to three million boxes of pluots, by his math.) Another estimated between four and six million boxes. Rod smiled and offered, "Two to eight million."

"You know what's interesting about the pluots is that their apricot nature sometimes comes out from a pest management point of view," the pest adviser said. "Some of them don't react to oil very well or to sulfur, which are two traits of apricots."

That was interesting, I said, especially since some people think there's no apricot in them at all.

"Yeah well, there's apricot in some of them. I can promise you that. The main problem with the pluots, as some of these guys will tell you, is that they can have setting problems."

"Flavorich, Flavorosa, Flavor Fall all have setting problems," Rod said. "When Flavorosa came out, it was like the second coming. It was big. It tasted as good as, if not better than, a Friar, and it had a consistent flavor no matter if it was big or small. It set real well in Modesto, but then it didn't set as well down here as it did up there. And then it cracked, too."

"With those early pluots, a lot of people went in big and got smacked around," said the pest adviser. "There's a certain psychological component to it. You see other people getting in on it and you want to get in on it, too."

I offered that I'd heard some people say that varieties should be completely vetted before they're released to growers.

"That's bullshit!" Rod said, then, softer, "Excuse me. But who's to say what's good for me in terms of varieties? What's good for me is going to be different than what's good for somebody else. I consider varietal selection the shear pin that determines who should be in this industry and who shouldn't. If you get rid of that shear pin, then everybody can do it. If I pick good varieties, then I stay in business. That's my edge."

"That's everything," agreed the pest adviser. "That's the *whole* thing. Every year, I've got guys I work with who say, 'I can't afford to plant new varieties.' And I say, 'No, you can't afford not to.' When you quit searching for new varieties, that's when they write your epitaph."

Later, as we were heading back toward Rod's place, I asked him again about varietal selection. We had discussed it before and nothing else we'd talked about had elicited such a strong response. It was always a risk to put in a new, experimental variety. Any number of things could go wrong with it. But if you saw something promising, it was a really good bet that plenty of others had seen it, too. And if that variety did take off, you wanted to be one of the first to have it. So there was a risk, as well, in not putting it in. "There's risk involved either way," Rod said, matter-of-factly. "But if you want someone to hold your hand and treat you like a baby, this just isn't the business for you. If you want certainty, go get a job at PG&E. Get in the business or get out, but stop whining."

And even though many of the interspecifics seemed more unstable, more unpredictable than established varieties, that was something that the grower had to be aware of going in. That had to be part of the grower's calculus as he figured out which varieties to grow.

"Like with Flavorosa. I was one of the very first growers to put it in. I had ten acres in before I knew it, and that was a big risk for me. And it drops a lot. And we have to pick it six or seven times, which adds to the labor costs. But overall it's been a big winner for me. Now, it's time to graft it out and I think I'm going to put in Flavor Royale as a replacement. *But that's what's right for me.* Somebody else may want to hold on to it and for somebody else it may not work at all."

He mentioned a newer Zaiger variety called Flavor Grenade. A smallish, oblong pluot with skin that mottles dull yellow to dull red, Flavor Grenade is a piece of fruit marketers describe as "unique" when what they mean is "ugly." It is also very sweet, which is why retailers have been more forgiving about its size and appearance. Flavor Grenade comes off the tree around the same time Friar does, and side-by-side there's no question which plum you'd rather eat. But since Rod already had a lot of Friars, and they were doing well in terms of sales, he couldn't justify pulling out the Friars to put in the Flavor Grenade.

"Sometimes you can look at the perfect piece of fruit and say, 'Man, *that* is a nice piece of fruit. But it just doesn't make sense for me.' And then if I've got five years left on these Friars, then in five years there's probably going to be something else coming along that's even better [than Flavor Grenade]. So it's a moving target."

Rod explained that you also had to think about logistics. If you had a variety you wanted to pull out, you had to think not just about what else you had going on during that part of the season. You had to think about what was adjacent to that part of your orchard. For example, you didn't want to put in a variety you'd have to pick mid-season next to a variety you'd have to spray mid-season. The spray could drift over and settle on the fruit. You had to consider the ground you'd be planting in; in general, peaches and nectarines were less forgiving of poor soil than plums were. If possible, you wanted to put a plum next to another plum that could act as a pollinator. And the list of considerations went on. "There are a ton of factors to consider and you can talk yourself into any number of them," Rod said.

One other thing Rod had to think about when choosing varieties was what Rick had planted in his orchard. Since they often shared a crew, they tried to coordinate on varieties so that they weren't too heavy during any one part of the season. We were headed to Rick's place now to see how his Grand Rosas were coming. When we pulled up to the house, the brothers' father, Richard, was sitting in his truck waiting for a load of the plums. At eighty-one, Richard was mostly retired but still hauled fruit over to Ballantine during the season.

While Rod went to check on the crew back at his place, I climbed into the passenger side of Richard's pickup. A trailer of Grand Rosas—Rick's last load—was on its way over. They took one load per hour over to Ballantine, four bins loaded with about a thousand pounds of Grand Rosas apiece. Right on cue, a tractor appeared with four bins. Richard got out and guided the bins onto the trailer hitched to his truck, and then we were off. We passed a field of artichokes, then some turnips and eggplants, and then turned into Ballantine's delivery entrance and stopped under a giant porte cochere. Richard unlatched the trailer, which tilted backward slightly from the weight. He leaned down and pushed the two back bins, causing the whole four thousand pounds worth of plums to slide down the trailer, then climbed back in the truck and eased it forward so that the last bins slid off. He went into a side office and picked up a receiving certificate, a yellow 5×8-inch card with his grower number and information on what and how much he'd brought in. While he did that, I watched a guy on a forklift zip around the loading area, moving fruit around. He speared the four Milton bins and carried them through a large freight door. Inside, the fruit would be sorted, sized, packed, and then, given the current state of the market, probably stuck in the cooler for a while.

As we unloaded, I asked Richard if he'd seen a market as bad as this one. "Well, I'm sure I have. But if agriculture had a brain in her head, she'd just say, 'No! Hell no!' It would take only a week and then the week after would be the most profitable week you'd ever see. The thing that is bad about our world today—and this is age talking here—is that we don't know how to say no to anything."

After our Grand Rosa run to Ballantine, Richard dropped me off at the old packing shed to his house. Rod was on his forklift, stacking some empty bins that had been dropped off from Ballantine. As Rod finished, a field manager from Ballantine pulled up. He'd stopped by to coordinate with Rod about the next several days. "On the Arctic Blaze [peaches]," he said, shaking his head, "we're just picking forty-eight and larger." Rod sighed. The field manager turned to me and said, "Last year, we sold out of seventy-twos."

Peach sizes are determined by how many pieces of fruit fit in the box. The smaller the number, the larger the fruit. Last year, they were able to sell out of smaller peaches. This year, they were backed up on fruit that was much larger. Not a good sign.

I asked the field manager what they did with the smaller fruit.

"You watch them fall to the ground," the field guy said. He shook his head and said, "This is definitely the worst year I've seen in my lifetime. I've never, ever seen it as bad as I've seen it this year."

"What is it about this year?"

"Nobody really knows. That's the worst part. But I think one thing is that the export market is way down," Rod said. "Some people think that's because they've had a real light typhoon season in Asia, so a lot of their local fruit is coming on in a way it normally doesn't.

"I think it's probably a lot of things like that," said the field manager. "You look at the buyers and you see that they're selling less fruit. They had sixty million boxes of stone fruit three years ago and now they've got forty-eight million, but they're not putting any of it on sale. They're selling less fruit for more.

"You've got incredible fruit and it's selling for thirty-nine cents a pound on the wholesale market in Los Angeles," said Rod. "When it's thirty-nine cents a pound in Los Angeles, you know you're in trouble."

The field guy shrugged and drove off, and I could tell Rod was eager to go check on his crew. I was planning to make some stops in Reedley before heading back to the hotel, but Rod told me to check back by the shed later. He'd see if he could get a box of fruit put together for me. "It's a little early for them, but I'll see if I can find some Flavor Kings that are ready."

A couple of hours later, I stopped at Rod's small shed and found a cardboard box filled with fruit. It was indeed a little early for the Flavor Kings—the first one crunched when I took a bite—but in a good year like this one, a slightly unripe Flavor King was better than most other plums at their best.

I was eating a second one in the car when I heard a radio ad for Von's. The grocery chain was promoting a big sale. It was for grapes.

2

BY AN ORDER of magnitude, Gerawan Farming is the largest stone fruit grower in the country. Ray Gerawan and his sons are notorious for keeping to themselves—except for when they don't keep to themselves, and then they're notorious for saying and doing things that a) infuriate, b) appear to belittle, and/or c) strike fear in fellow stone fruit growers. Legendary stories about the Gerawans' disinterest in tact float around the Valley. They are best known for a series of incendiary statements they made in various courts and hearings, the gist of which could be summed up in Ray's public claim that his "goal as a businessman was to put [his] competitors out of business." Their strain of rational self-interest was pure and their promotion of laissez-faire principles was never sugarcoated. (If Ayn Rand had written a novel about fruit growing, she could have found no better Objectivist hero than Ray Gerawan.)

The Gerawans had led the charge against the Plum Marketing Board in the early 1990s and eventually convinced enough plum growers to vote themselves out of the federal marketing order. Once the plum growers voted themselves back into the mandatory marketing order at the state level, the Gerawans sued the Plum Marketing Board in state court. In fact, many people speculated that the reason the California Department of Food and Agriculture had refused to intervene in the pluot issue was because the Gerawans had kept the state so tangled in legal battles that it was afraid to weigh in on any new issue that involved peaches, plums, or nectarines. During my time in the Valley, I heard all kinds of words used to describe Ray Gerawan, and none of them was flattering. That made it all the more impressive that I never once heard a bad word about the Gerawans' fruit. The company's Prima brand was the premier plum label in the industry. People talked about its consistently high quality with something approaching reverence.

I'd heard so much about Ray Gerawan that I couldn't imagine not meeting the man. After a series of phone calls with his son Dan, I found myself on the way to Ray's house one Sunday afternoon. On the eastern side of Reedley, I passed Gerawan Farming's main packing facility, a big rectangular fortress. I cut north and drove almost to where the road hit the foothills. Tall evergreens out front hid a beautiful, low 1960s hacienda-style ranch. A tall, handsome man in his seventies answered the door. He was on the phone, speaking Spanish. He nodded and motioned for me to follow him inside. The inside was airy and open but barely lit. We walked to a sunroom in the back of the house, where he sat at a table and finished his conversation. In an ashtray, a Marlboro Light was burning down. He lit another and hung up the phone.

"I'm learning more Spanish."

"A good language to know."

"So you're interested in stone fruit breeders?" He'd had enough of the chitchat. "I've put hundreds of thousands—millions—of dollars into patent payments and replantings and variety changes," he said evenly. "They should do more testing and somebody should take them to court to hold them accountable so that they make sure the varieties do the things they say they're going to do." He blew out a long line of smoke in my general direction.

Ray's family moved from Oklahoma when he was five. His father bought forty acres of land near the foothills, land that "even God didn't want." The family grew a little bit of everything. Santa Rosa plums. Elberta peaches. Grapes. Okra. Ray began working by digging ditches, picking fruit, walking behind a mule. A year after he finished high school, he bought his first ranch. He had good years and bad years, dabbling in this and that. By the 1970s, he had built up a big stone fruit business that prized volume over quality. He picked every piece of fruit he could get into the box. If somebody would buy it, he would pack it.

When he was in his mid-forties, his wife left him, and the separation prompted a Siddhartha-like walkabout. Every morning for two years, he woke up and walked up into the foothills to wander and think. One morning, he ran across a Canadian hiker, and the two men started talking about life. After listening to Ray for a while, the hiker remarked that his philosophy of life reminded him of Khalil Gibran's *The Prophet*. When Ray returned home, he bought the book, and it was partly responsible for his return to the workaday life of growing and packing stone fruit. His sons had all but taken over the company and, with his blessing, they were shifting the focus of Gerawan Farming from quantity to quality. This was around the same time that the hegemony of the Big Eight was breaking up, and it was a good time to make the change.

The Prophet became Ray's Bible. "It's very important to me now," he said, pointing to a bound copy on the table and breathing out another long line of smoke. "And he was Lebanese, like I am."

I mentioned the CTFA lawsuit and his public statements about the industry. How did his philosophy of business mesh with Gibran?

"My philosophy is survival of the fittest. In this family, we're real big on free enterprise. As I told the federal attorney, my philosophy *is* to try to put my competitors out of business. And when I said that, I meant it as a challenge to my competitors to try to put me out of business. Because that makes us all stronger."

"Do you socialize with anybody in the business?"

"No!"

"Is it because you don't want to socialize with people who you're trying to put out of business?"

"No, it's not that. The reason why I don't socialize with them is because all these guys want to talk about is fruit. Fruit, fruit, fruit, fruit, fruit, fruit, fruit. It's not that I hate fruit. It's just that I'm saturated by it."

"Are you sympathetic to the plight of the small guys out there who are going out of business?"

"Do I sound like I'd be sympathetic to that? Do I sound like I'm sympathetic to anything?"

"But what about the value of having competition? Isn't it good to have lots of competition?"

He shook his head. "The plum deal is finished anyway. It's a much harder pack. The buyers want a fixed quantity for the year and won't come down on price. They're not willing to come up on volume."

It was the same thing I'd been hearing from everybody else.

A few days later, I met Ray for breakfast at the Main Street Cafe, in Reedley. He wanted me to meet Russ Tavlan, a young, like-minded guy who ran his own farming company. When I showed up, Ray was sitting at a table up front, talking on his cell phone. He gave me a quick nod and then went back to his phone conversation for a few more minutes until Russ showed up.

"I just talked to John," Ray said to Russ, "and got the price down two dollars a box so that I could move the fruit on the street." John was a wholesaler on the East Coast. The market was still way down and fruit was stacking up in cold storage facilities all across the Valley. By cutting the price for the wholesaler, Ray was open to clearing a lot of fruit out of cold storage, which would bring the market back up for the first several weeks of August.

"Why did you do that?" Russ demanded. "You devalued one of your quality retail partners. These are the guys that butter your bread, and you've just come off two dollars." The wholesaler did occasional business with some of the same retailers with whom Gerawan dealt directly. Russ was concerned that by lowering the price for the wholesaler, Ray would be in danger of competing with himself.

"So?"

"So? Well, number one: It's proven that two dollars isn't enough to move volume. Number two: I don't believe this theory that there's a correlation between retail and street. Anyway, I sent him an e-mail last night and wrote: 'You better pull some Prima nectarine or Ray Gerawan's going to cut your balls off.' "

Ray looked at me and smiled. "I've been training him."

"I've been training *him!*" Russ shot back. "I'm keeping him tethered to society."

To Russ, Ray said, "Chip's been hearing bad things about me in the industry."

Russ nodded and said, "The industry loves to hate Gerawan. It's systemic in Gerawan that it doesn't seem to make any mistakes. People just can't believe the consistent quality. That's what distinguishes them. The first box looks the same as the box fifty thousand boxes later."

Russ's cell phone rang. It was John. Russ answered and said, "We gonna do business, you parasite?"

After he hung up, Russ said, "Ray's got people who *need* Gerawan Farming. It's a different paradigm. You've got regional and national chains whose whole programs are based on the Prima label. A place like Kingsburg Orchards has built their entire business on niches. Gerawan has built his business on mainstream varieties."

Ray, who was eating strawberry jelly with the tip of a knife, kept silent, and Russ looked at me solemnly. "Listen, Ray's never sought the limelight, but he's also never shied away from saying what's on his mind. And that's a rarity in this business. When I was getting going, he said, 'Russ, if you do this, your only goal should be to put me out of business. That's your only goal. If it's not, then get the fuck out right now!' "

Ray pointed at me and said, "That's 'g-e-t . . . ' " His phone interrupted him. He answered and went back to haggling over nectarines.

As Russ half-listened to Ray's conversation, he explained that times like this were why he loved stone fruit. "It's the fastest-paced crop, and the tight-knit family business has the ability to react faster than any big corporation. What you get in agriculture outside of stone fruit, it's a world dominated by large, global enterprises. But in stone fruit, the big corporations have come and gone."

I asked Russ what he thought was going on with the market.

"The supply is surpassing any of our expectations. The fruit quality is incredible. It's everything we strive for. But there's too much of it."

"In a market like this, does the need for an organization like the CTFA become more apparent?"

"Of course not!" Ray had hung up the phone and heard me ask Russ the question. "I don't believe there's any benefit to any associations of any kind at any time."

"Ray likes to hit you over the head with a bag of nickels and see how you react," Russ said to me. "He's the Howard Stern of the fruit business."

"More like the Howard Hughes," I said.

"Well, maybe a little bit of both."

3

WHILE THE WRANGLING over the pluot's identity sometimes made it seem as if the Zaigers were the only stone fruit breeders in town, they had plenty of competition. In addition to the breeders working at the universities and at the USDA, Gerawan had its own in-house breeding program, which, judging by the consistently good quality of its fruit, seemed to be a success. Another large farming company called Sun World International had a proprietary plum breeding program that was built on the work of a legendary breeder named John Weinberger, who had introduced, among other things, the Flame Seedless grape. The Zaigers' main rival, though, was Bradford Genetics, the modern incarnation of Fred Anderson's breeding operation in Le Grand.

Norman Bradford, now retired in his eighties, had worked most of his life as Fred Anderson's field manager. When Anderson retired, Norman and his son Glen bought the ranch and continued the breeding program. The Zaigers and Bradfords were cordial and cooperative but kept a respectable distance from each other. Patent law made it illegal to use pollen from someone else's protected varieties. The Zaigers and Bradfords also had a gentleman's agreement not to use each other's unpatented cultivars.

Having continued the work of the Father of the Modern Nectarine, the Bradfords were known mostly for their work with that fruit. But in the past decade, they had begun impressing a lot of people with their plums. Just as the Zaigers used Red Beaut, an old Anderson variety, as one of the foundations of their pluot line, the Bradfords based most of their plums on an old red-fleshed Anderson cultivar that had been on the ranch when they bought it. The Bradfords' foundation plum, like Red Beaut, was a direct descendant of one of Burbank's original twelve Japanese plums, probably the Blood Plum of Satsuma (according to Burbank, the Blood Plum was the only of his original red-fleshed Japanese plums he continued to use as his breeding program progressed).

Unlike the Zaigers, Glen Bradford did all his crossing in the field. When he wanted to cross plums, he built small houses around the trees. Inside, he stuck a small hive of bees and set blossoming branches in a bowl of water. Like the Zaigers, he too hybridized plums with apricots and backcrossed with plumcots. But having followed the scuffle over the word "pluot," he decided just to call his hybrids by a simpler name: *plums*.

Glen gave his own fruit tour every Tuesday morning during the season. The morning I went, there were a dozen or so people there, including several guys from Bright Brothers Nursery, which was the production arm of Bradford Genetics that propagated and sold the varieties the Bradfords developed and took a commission on each tree. There were also a couple of growers and some packing shed reps, plus a woman who worked for Top Fruit, the Bradfords' exclusive partner in South Africa.

We set out on foot, and like everywhere else, the conversation quickly turned to the down market. People here had reached the same frustrated conclusions I'd heard elsewhere. The numbers were "devastating." Many buyers "didn't have a clue about the fruit business." Much of the fruit in storage "should go into the Dumpster." In a lot of packers' coolers, "you had to back out to just to move around."

Glen wondered aloud whether people might just be sick of eating bad fruit. "Two of my daughters won't even touch plums," he said. "It's the same thing as 'I burned my hand with a firecracker once.' After that, you don't want to go near firecrackers again." It lightened the mood a little to hear those words come out of the mouth of one of the world's top plum breeders. There weren't a lot of plums on the tour because most of them were tied up in an exclusive arrangement Glen had going with Mike Jackson and Kingsburg Orchards. In one sweeping deal capped by a handshake, Glen ceded Kingsburg Orchards his entire inventory of red-fleshed plums. No other California grower could have the red-fleshed plums—not even David and those other Jacksons at Family Tree Farms. (Glen had also given Kingsburg Orchards an exclusive on the black apricot that had sent David circumnavigating the globe on the hunt for flavor.)

Out in the orchard, Glen moved quickly from one tree to another. A mechanical engineer by training who'd fallen into the family business, he wasn't the kind of guy you'd ever hear quoting Basho on the reticence of blossoms. As we walked around sampling varieties, here, too, were the same jokes about watermelons, cantaloupes, and rogue fruits. After tasting a July Bright nectarine, someone said, "Careful, it's got a little kick to it." Somebody else fired back, "Does that mean it's good for France?" As I walked around, tasting, testing, putting fruit in my tote sack, I thought about an underlined passage in our copy of William Gass's *In the Heart of the Heart of the Country*. (Elizabeth was the one who'd underlined it—I can tell by the way the line curves and thins out from left to right.) In the preface, Gass wrote, "Nature rarely loops. Nature repeats. This spring is not a former spring rethought, but merely another spring, somewhat the same, somewhat not." This was a different COC List than the ones I'd paced off at the Zaigers' place. These were different people and a different time, but the movements repeated, somewhat the same, somewhat not.

At one point, I hopped in a cart with a grower named Rob Mazuna, who has an unkempt ten-acre orchard near the foothills in Reedley. (His land abuts one of Gerawan's ranches.) Rob counts his varieties not in acres but in trees, as in "I've got thirty-four trees of Arctic Rose," a sublime white-flesh, sub-acid nectarine developed by the Zaigers. He sells his fruit once a week at a Sunday farmer's market several hours away in Mountain View (incidentally the hometown of Google). Rob comes to the Bradfords' every week, mostly for the camaraderie. Occasionally, he picks fruit from Glen's trees to take with him several days later to the market. Today, for example, he planned to clean off a couple of albino peach trees which Glen had already shown. If he didn't pick it, the fruit would just drop to the ground. Plus it was exactly the kind of thing that would sell at the market; the peaches were very soft, a little overripe, juicy, and melting. As we picked the fruit into a couple of boxes, Rob explained that at the farmer's market, their being overripe didn't matter. Size didn't matter. Color didn't matter either. "Elberta has no color. Flavor Gold has no color," taking mental inventory of some of his duller varieties. Most of the things on the farmer-friendly checklist didn't matter, because the fruit didn't have to speak for itself at the farmer's market. Rob could speak for it. He could chat up the people there, slice them a sample, talk to them about the history of the variety and why he planted it. He could prime the customer and then let the fruit close the deal, so the only thing that mattered was the eating experience, the flavor. Rob's ten acres were wallowing in that. His orchard was like a COC List of the COC List, stone fruit's greatest hits—Zaiger varieties mixed in with Bradford varieties, old-school Elberta peaches, tropical-tasting plums.

"I just plant what I like and when it's time to pick for the market, I pick what's ready. My wife doesn't like me to waste the fruit. She wants me to get a cold storage unit. To me though, that's like having a hot dog warmer. You know, you make all these hot dogs at Seven-Eleven and then you put them in that thing to keep them warm? If you have that thing to keep them warm, then you just get in the habit of making the hot dogs ahead of time. So, I use what I can and dump whatever I can't sell."

I thought about what one grower had said to me, that growing stone fruit had gone from being a lifestyle to being a business. Rob's operation wasn't much of a business. It wasn't even much of a lifestyle. It was more like a beautiful, ten-acre art project. By the time we finished picking the albino peach, the tour was over and some of the guys were carpooling to lunch.

Glen had an errand to run and he seemed a little anxious to get to it. When I got in his truck, he told me why. Mike Watts, Kingsburg Orchards' Director of Exotic Fruit, had called Glen the day before and asked if he could swing by on his way up to a meeting with an upscale regional chain based in Modesto. The chain mostly carried Gerawan's Prima label, and Watts wanted to blow open a new account by giving them a taste of some of the exclusive red-fleshed plums Kingsburg Orchards had on the horizon. The trees Kingsburg Orchards had growing were too young and not yet setting fruit, so Mike had asked Glen to pick a handful of boxes for him to take. We were going to meet Mike at an unmarked turnoff of Highway 99. Glen had half a dozen small boxes in the back, filled gently with fruit. Just off the northbound side of 99, we pulled off into the shade of an almond orchard.

"Have you had people gripe about the exclusive with the Jacksons?" I asked him.

He raised his eyebrows and said, "Here and all over the world." While we waited, Glen told me how "the red-fleshed plum thing" with Kingsburg Orchards had come about. Because Bradford had been known for so long as a nectarine outfit, no one had really given their plums much of a chance. In the mid-1990s, they'd developed a line of red-fleshed plums, and had begun marketing them in their nursery catalog. But no one had been interested, in part because plums had fallen so far out of favor with growers and in part because pluots were just taking off at that point and were getting all the plum-related attention. So Glen had just moved on and kind of forgotten about them, until Kingsburg Orchards had approached him one day about doing exclusives.

Right around this time, some studies had come out about the antioxidant power of red-fleshed plums, and since no one had shown much interest in the Bradfords' inventory, they had taken the plums to the Jacksons and said, "Want an exclusive on these?" That was several years ago now, and though none of the plums had made it out into the market yet, Glen was happy with the arrangement. Instead of taking a commission on every tree the nursery sold, Glen would get a percentage of Kingsburg Orchards' revenue off the fruit. And because the plums were exclusive to Kingsburg Orchards, the Jacksons could control volume and marketing of the whole line. There were no fears of overplanting a variety or having it picked too soon so that it showed up in stores hard and green.

Eventually, Mike Watts pulled up in a BMW and jumped out of the car almost before it stopped. He was wearing a Hawaiian shirt, red and pink with yellow flowers on it, and the effulgence fit his mood. We carried the boxes over to him, and he opened the first one and took out a piece of fruit, a small, dark purplish plum covered in chalky bloom.

"Mike!" His wife, Brenda, had rolled down the window. "Stop that!"

He turned and smiled at her. "But I've got to eat it! I need to know what it's going to taste like." He leaned forward and took a bite. "Oh!" He made a little kick. "Oh! This one is dizzy!" He waved his hand to find the right word. "Oh, it's, it's, it's dizzy-sweet. It's choke-sweet!" He was nodding at Glen for an acknowledgment of this phrase. "It hits the back of your throat and it chokes you! Here, Brenda. Try this."

Brenda took off her seat belt and got out of the car. "He's like a kid with a new toy."

Mike had opened another box and was trying a different plum. "Oh my god! You have to eat this. Brenda! Here! Eat this!" He thrust the plum toward her.

"I can't eat them both at the same time, Mike!"

"Oh, that is so sweet!" He spun around in a circle.

We loaded the boxes into the backseat of the BMW, and then the Wattses were gone as quickly as they'd come, like a three-gag Vaudeville act between sets.

4

W E CAN DELIVER the best box of fruit in the world, but
at the end of the day, it's the guys in the green aprons—
the guys who are stocking the fruit in the store—who are the
gatekeepers. And as an industry, we have no contact with them."

David Jackson was mulling this problem over in a small club
chair in the sitting area of Family Tree Farms' sales and marketing department. Through a large window, he could look across
the street and check on the progress of the golf course. Sprin-
klers were now watering great expanses of sod. The occasional
tree broke the landscape, and in the distance, construction on
the clubhouse was under way.

Like Blair Richardson and FreshSense, Family Tree was always trying to figure out how to reach farther into the store to
better market its fruit. They'd been scheming about it for years.
Finally, one day, somebody at Family Tree hatched the brilliant
idea of bringing the store to them. Just like that, Flavor Tech
was born: a two-day, round-the-clock cram session designed for
produce managers and buyers from Family Tree's retail partners. "We wanted to show those guys in the green aprons what

it takes to make a piece of fruit. So we bring a group of them out and cover things like the difference between taste and flavor, how we process flavor, the psychology of a purchase, all those kinds of things. They leave here with a diploma and their chests are pumped up. Then, they go home and they talk. And we see sales jump in those stores."

This morning, half a dozen produce managers from a regional chain in the Midwest were coming to town for Flavor Tech, but their flight had been delayed out of Chicago and they were running an hour or two late. With some time to kill, I drove around Dinuba.

Right outside of town, there was a big, new development going in, Sugar Plum Estates. (If suburbs elsewhere were often named for the natural thing they had replaced, in the Valley they were often named for the crop that had already replaced the natural thing.) Since my last visit, a new retail cluster had sprung up on the perimeter of Dinuba's Wal-Mart Supercenter, which itself was only a year old. When the cluster was finished, there would be a Krogen Auto Parts, a Dollar Tree, and some species of quickie mart. Whenever I was in the orbit of a Wal-Mart Supercenter, I liked to run in and check the produce. Today, the very first thing visible in the store was a massive, detached rack of black plums with a sign announcing that they were on sale for $1.00 per pound. (Usually, they were $1.74.) Some of them were labeled with the 4039 PLU stickers: small plums. Others were 4040s, normal-size plums. I hovered for fifteen or twenty minutes, watching to see if anyone went for the plums. No one did. Most people didn't even seem to notice them. They could have been invisible. The rest of the produce selection loomed beyond the plums, and in the much smaller bin of pluots, there were a few different varieties represented, including some early Dapple Dandies. The pluots were $2.94 per pound. Aside from some dark cherries that were a little over $3.00 per pound, the pluots were the most expensive item in the produce section. I bought a couple of plums and a couple of pluots, and sat in the parking lot eating them. They could have used a day in a paper sack to ripen, but all of them tasted pretty good. I still hadn't had a bad plum all summer.

When I got back to Family Tree, the produce managers were still on the way from the Fresno airport, so I sat down to chat with Family Tree's marketing director, a stone fruit lifer named Don Goforth. Don had been in the business for twenty-five years and was active in the Produce Marketing Association, the national trade organization that, among other things, doled out PLU numbers. (He'd sat on the board that reviewed the request for a "pluot" code.) He'd probably thought about marketing stone fruit as much as anyone on the planet, and he'd come around to the opinion that the word "pluot" was not cutting it.

Lately, his team had been getting some resistance from retailers over the name. Some of it was familiar territory from the Interspecific Task Force days and the "if it walks like a duck" debate. What exactly was a pluot? How was it different than a plum? This resistance was especially frustrating because the marketers had really been trying to brand the word "pluot" as something new and different, hoping that it would leapfrog some of the negative feelings people had about plums and get the consumer to associate the word with a perception of better flavor. Anecdotally, the word was said to have caught on in some "foodie" circles, but the stores were also reporting a lot of confusion on the consumer end, a sign that the word had not penetrated far enough. Another problem was that all those high-flavor interspecific plums that Family Tree had gotten from the overseas breeders couldn't be called "pluots," because the word was a trademark owned by the Zaigers. And so the word they were pushing as the new and better thing could never be as inclusive as it needed to be.

There was another, more fundamental issue, and it was with the word itself—namely, it's not obvious how to pronounce "pluot" just by looking at it. It's one of only six words in the English language that ends in the letters "-uot." There aren't too many more words with that sequence of letters anywhere. By Merriam-Webster's count, there are sixty-six of them, and in all but just a few, the "u" is preceded by a "q" and is silent—as in "quote." But in "pluot," the "u" counts, and the tendency is to go French with the second syllable, as I first did when I asked the guy at the farmer's market what the deal was with the "plew-ohs." Even if you know that the word is a merger of "plum" and "apricot," the sound doesn't make much sense, because the "u" in "plum" is short while the "u" in "pluot" is long. "Pluot" looks like a word someone's left a letter out of. When I told Don about all the grocery store displays I'd seen—plucots, plumots, plouts—he nodded. He'd seen them, too.

"We've really pushed the word 'pluot'—not just Family Tree, others in the industry, too—but when people can't pronounce it, it's tough to get it to stick. You're always trying to tell people that it's a cross between a plum and an apricot, but it's hard to see that in the name. In just looking at the name, there's no way to even tell that it's a food."

There was a growing sense then that, as a brand, "pluot" was neither functional nor evocative. In response, Don said, there was talk among industry marketers of lumping all high-flavor, interspecific plums into a category called "plumcots." Since Burbank's days, the word "plumcot" had been used almost exclusively to describe fifty-fifty crosses between plums and apricots, like the Zaigers' early hybrid, Flavorella. But nowhere was it written that a plumcot had to be fifty-fifty, and so the word was getting a lot of attention as a possible catchall. "It's a *better* word," said Don. "What it is is right there in the name. We've done some informal consumer surveys and people have said, '*Plumcot* I can understand. *Pluot* makes no sense.' And as much as we like to think otherwise, in reality, 'pluot' doesn't have enough traction for us not to say, 'Hey, we can rename this and start to call it a 'plumcot.'" Though its existence was little known and it was almost never used, the plumcot did have its own PLU code: 3126. If the industry could get the same color breakdown as plums had—red plumcots, black plumcots, and so on—then the whole high-flavor, interspecific marketing issue might be at least partially resolved. After all the task forces and hearings, they could retire the word "pluot" once and for all.

"From there, you could work on flavor profiles," he said. "'This tastes like that,' and so on, so that you can have people excited about a whole line of fruit that you can work into your programs."

The eight produce managers had just arrived from the airport in Fresno, and Don went in to greet them. The group moved into a conference room and said their hellos. The produce managers were from places like Davenport, Iowa; Omaha, Nebraska; and Rochester, Minnesota. They were a hardy bunch, and they'd all been working for the regional chain for at least a decade, many of them two. As they introduced themselves, they sounded the same alarm: "Wal-Mart's hurting us" or "Wal-Mart opened up against us two years ago" or "Wal-Mart's the heaviest competition but we're holding pretty strong." It felt like a brigadier's report from the Mongol front.

Don gave a short spiel on Family Tree—family owned, Christian values, vertically integrated—and then summed up the point of Flavor Tech. "We believe that if we grow good fruit, we will be successful. We're committed to the satisfaction of the end consumer, and so with us, it's all about flavor. It's that simple." There were nods around the table. That *was* simple.

Don looked around the table and continued his spiel without notes. "We sell a product that tells a story. Without confidence, none of us is willing to talk about anything. I can't go to Boston and talk about the Red Sox, right? Those guys know what they're talking about and I don't. So too often we don't say anything if we don't feel confident about it. That's just human nature. One time, I was on the East Coast and I went up to a kid who was stacking potatoes and onions. His name was Billy. I said, 'Billy, how often do you talk to the customers?' Billy looked up and said, 'All she represents to me is an interruption between my potatoes and my onions. Not only that, she's just going to ask me a question I can't answer.'" Don paused. "That's a problem." More nods around the table.

Over the next hour, Don gave a concise and often rousing

presentation on the California stone fruit industry. He had several slides on the nuts and bolts of interspecifics. When he came to a slide with the words "Genus: Prunus" and a picture of peaches, plums, nectarines, apricots, and cherries, Don smiled and said, "I think of these as all dogs. Different types of dogs, but they're all dogs. Well, you can't breed a dog with a cat. You can put them in the same room with all the candlelight and white wine in the world, but it's not going to work: you can't get a cat-dog. But you can cross the fruits in *Prunus*, because even though they're different, they're all dogs." More nods. All dogs.

The second day of Flavor Tech started on one of Family Tree's ranches in Goshen, down near Visalia. When I arrived, David Jackson was showing the produce managers his Flavor Queens, which he kept as the pollinator for a newer, yellow pluot called Sweet Treat. With his shadow on the field, David seemed totally in his element—a solid block of enthusiasm.

We hopped into trucks and drove down a dirt road to a plot of Dapple Dandies. (The chain where the produce managers worked got most, if not all, of their Dapple Dandies from Kingsburg Orchards; the day before, one of them had said that the fruit his customers most often asked for by name was the Dinosaur Egg. David had forced a smile.) David pulled a piece of fruit off the tree. "It's kind of been the history of this variety that we pick one, two, three, sometimes even four weeks later than a lot of companies pick this variety. But even though we have the most planted, our warehouse is sold out and cleaned before theirs are. It's one principle that we live by and it's going to work for all of us: If you give the housewife a good product, it'll move and keep moving. If you give her a bad product, she'll pick it up once and then three weeks later she'll start thinking about buying it again." This was the data that John Lundeen had compiled. "A sixteen-Brix Dapple Dandy is a good Dapple Dandy. It's an older Zaiger variety, and it's the backbone variety that started us into pluots. We're just now generations beyond it. The next generation is eighteen Brix and up. The stuff I'm going to show you later today, we're bringing in from Israel, France, Australia as well as taking from the plant breeders here in California. This stuff is bricking at twenty-two, twenty-three. I even have some twenty-nine Brix stuff. It'll render you unconscious if you don't have water with you."

We were standing on the edge of eighty acres of Dapple Dandy. At one time, David had forty acres of Flavor King and forty acres of Dapple Dandy, alternating every two rows for pollination. "I don't know if you've ever tasted Flavor King, but they named it right. Until just recently, I considered it the best pluot or plum that I'd ever tasted. It's one of the sweetest, juiciest plums I've ever had, but it cracks on the bottom. So unfortunately, you can't grow it commercially. I tried for a long time but I couldn't stay with it. So we pulled all but two rows and made the rest Dapple Dandy."

We caravaned back to the main road, where David's son Rick was waiting for us on a tractor that was hitched to a trailer lined with a few benches. We climbed up onto the benches, and while Rick drove, David narrated. At one point deep in the orchard, we stopped to watch a guy on a tractor top two rows of Flavor Fall. The brace of the topper sat on a trailer behind the tractor. It was shaped like an inverted "L" and it held a spinning circular blade that sheared the tops of the trees into flattops. Topping trees after the fruit had been picked allowed more light to get down into the branches, which was thought to help renew the trees after the growing season. Some people did it. Some people didn't.

As we pulled over to watch the topper, we noticed a group of men talking in a tight circle in front of a small house. The Jacksons liked to provide houses on the ranch for some of the higher-ups in the field. During the season, they were out in the trees around the clock, and so it helped to be sleeping close enough to the fruit to hear it fall. They also had a better chance of seeing their families once in a while. It was jarring, though, to see a house plopped down in the middle of thousands of acres of fruit trees. "This is somebody's home?" one of the produce managers asked. "Yeah, Gustavo lives here. He's a three-star."

I'd overheard this but I wasn't sure if I'd heard correctly.

"Did you say three-star?"

"They probably saw J. R. pulling up and had a meeting to get it together." In the field, it turned out, the Jacksons used a military-style system of rank. The field managers were three-stars. The "Hondas" were the guys on ATVs who coordinated with the work crews out in the field and reported back to the three-stars. J. R. Martinez, who ran farming operations for the entire ranch, was the equivalent of a four-star, though Family Tree didn't extend the military rank system beyond the lieutenants. As J. R. approached us David asked him what the meeting was about.

"Well, we were just telling them that there was a lot of the season left and we needed to be taking better care of the fruit. A lot of people were driving too fast, and there was a lot of fruit getting spilled out in the field."

Eventually, we pulled back around to the lot off Highway 99 where we'd left our cars, next to a barnish-looking structure that was in the middle of construction. "This is our top-secret R&D facility," David said, "and it's right off the busiest highway in California." When completed, the building would be a combination lab and tasting room. It was surrounded by ten acres of experimental test blocks. This is where Family Tree tested new Zaiger and Bradford varieties, as well as the foreign trees that were coming out of quarantine. We walked inside the unfinished building, where a couple of guys were working on the walls above us with drills and nail guns.

Rick found an empty box and tossed it to the center of the room. David brought out a dozen paper bags with numbers scribbled in marker across the side. "We've been talking a lot about Brix," he said. "It's really more than that. It's about the sugar-to-acid ratio. A lemon can have sixteen Brix, but you can't taste the sugar because there's too much acid. Okay? So it's the sugar-acid ratio that's important. That affects flavor." He mentioned an emulsifier he'd seen in Germany that could give a quick read on a fruit's sugar-acid ratio. He was thinking about investing in one, so that he could come closer to guaranteeing a good piece of fruit. "I want to be able to stamp on the box—boom!—'Guaranteed good eating experience!'"

The produce managers and I had formed a loose huddle around him. By this point, each of us was, I think, making a mental note to send him a résumé. He leaned down and peeked into one of the paper bags, and then picked it up and passed it around.

"Here's a little piece of fruit. This is a Zaiger variety. It's new. It isn't out yet. Just take a bite. You don't have to eat the whole thing. It's got a little tropical flavor to it."

It was a small, reddish-purple pluot. Everybody took a bite. I heard several of the guys say, "Oh!" They exchanged looks. *Poor bastards*, I thought. *Just wait.*

"Does it eat alright?" David said, serious, then breaking out into a smile. "Yeah! So there you go. That's probably in the twenties. Maybe twenty-one. You were eating sixteens out there. This is ramped up a little bit."

"What's that one called?" someone asked.

"It's not called anything yet. It's just got an identification number from the breeder. So we'll taste something like this and if we think it has real potential, next year we'll get six trees of it. It'll go here in the experimental farm and our guy will research and develop it out to see if it's something we can invest in."

"How long do you usually test a variety before putting in lots of trees?" I asked.

By way of answering, David picked up another bag, which held ten or so pieces of a small, squat nectarine from Glen Bradford. "I ate this one the other day and I ordered ten acres on the spot. So, I guess I tested it for about . . ."—he took a bite—"that long! And in those ten acres I'll have a lot of wood, so if they do well, I can expand pretty quick."

We went through some apricots, a couple more nectarines, a peach or two. Then David picked up a small box a few feet away. "Okay, this is one I've been saving for you. This is what I consider to be the best plum in the world. It's from Israel. Unfortunately, it's about six weeks old. I've had it in my refrigerator, not in cold storage. I knew you were coming and I wanted to save you one each. The firmer ones are probably the best, but even on those, the skin wasn't as tart when they were ready to eat."

He held the box and we each took a plum. They were the size of racquetballs. The skin was dark purple, delicate, and wrinkly, like a prune. Bitten, it revealed bright red, almost purplish flesh. The smell jumped up and mugged you. The taste was not a gentle, velvety sweet. It was fierce, spicy. You wouldn't want to saddle a child with it. It was an adult dose. One of the produce managers said only, "That—!" and then didn't finish the sentence. The guy next to me looked over and shook his head, and I recognized the look, because I'd felt myself give it so many times. It said, *After this, what?* I noticed that there was a piece of paper in the box and it had the number of the variety written on it. I wanted to know what this was—did it have a name?—but David noticed, and before I could copy down the number, he reached down, snatched up the paper, and put it in his pocket. He smiled at me and it was a tight, not entirely friendly smile.

"This is well past its time, but you can see what's there. When that thing is ready, you won't believe it. We've got a whole line of this coming. The same guy who did the red wine test and said that red wine is good for your heart and all that? Well, he tested this red juice and he said that they have four times the antioxidants that pomegranates have. So if we could have a line of these on your shelf that tastes like this all season long, and we can put a sign that says, 'Four times the antioxidants as pomegranate juice?' Put a price tag on that baby and let's sell it. See all those young trees out there?" He pointed beyond us. "Those are all that plum right there. From all those sticks on those small trees, we can go to a lot of acreage really fast."

Someone mentioned the size of the fruit and whether or not that might be a marketing challenge. David explained that since Israel exported most of its fruit to Europe (where small sells), Israeli growers didn't do much thinning to increase fruit size. Because there was so little water in Israel, their irrigation methods could also affect fruit size. "We're hoping that the size is a cultural thing and not genetic." (I thought of Burbank's bringing over the twelve seedlings from Japan and speculating that they would "respond to the stimulus of new surroundings.") "Because if the size is a genetic thing, then all of a sudden we've got to come together and say, 'Okay, we've got the best-tasting fruit in the world, but how are we going to sell this? Because Americans want it big.'"

David, who was returning to Israel the next week to order more fruit, continued flipping through the catalogue. He pointed out some apricots he had in the works: a black apricot, a striped "tiger" apricot, and a line they were calling *aromacots*, one of which had the smell of ginger bred into it. "This is all going on in the desert there in Israel. When I was there last was when they were sending the bombs over from Lebanon. Bombs hit two doors down. You know, we're out there picking and there's bombs going on in the hills, and the breeder said, 'I guess I should get these pickers out of here, but I really need to get that fruit off.' So that's what's coming from Israel now. This fall, we're getting thirty of them out of quarantine. And then we're getting thirty more the next year. And I'll probably order another thirty this year."

He showed us other catalogues, from Spain, from France, from Chile. As we passed and flipped through them, David became solemn. "The most important thing I do as a farmer is right here. Yes, we have to do all the cultural things right. The fruit has to be packed right. It has to be shipped right. But the most important thing I do is choose varieties. If I choose a variety that bricks fourteen and another guy chooses a variety that bricks twenty-one, then I can be the best farmer in the world and he can screw up every which way but loose. He'll still come out with a better product than me. So this research farm where we're standing represents what's most important to me."

He looked at us all—the half-time gut check—and smiled. "And just think! Next time you come here, there will be a long table over there and everything we've grown from the first of the season until where we're at now will be out on a plate, cut up for you to taste. And if you taste one and say, 'Egah! I like that one! I've got to have that one in the store,' then I'll say, 'Well you name it, man! How many acres you want?'" He laughed that high-pitched laugh, and it sounded crazy and brilliant.

5

MIKE JACKSON HAD his uncle Dave's laugh; I'd heard it over the telephone. In all the time I'd spent in the Valley, though, the closest I'd come to visiting Kingsburg Orchards and meeting him was driving along the outskirts of Jackson-owned land on Highway 43, where their trees were surrounded by tall razor-wire fence covered with a flowering vine. Over time, I'd tried to set up appointments with Mike and his father, George. Something always seemed to come up. But when Mike mentioned on a phone call that they still had the original Dapple Dandy test block that Wayne Adams had grafted in back in the 1980s, I vowed to get over there before leaving California.

I had come to think of Dapple Dandy (marketed by Kingsburg Orchards as Dinosaur Egg) as the first real action in the war on "big, red, and hard." If Flavor King was the Boston tea party of California stone fruit, then Dapple Dandy was the shot heard 'round the world. In my mind, those first trees had a talismanic quality to them. They were the bridge between the dark days of the recent past, when growers neglected to taste fruit because flavor was so low on the list of priorities, and the red-fleshed future, which was full of flavor.

On the day I was going to see Mike, it was blazing out; at 1:30 P.M., the car was a box of heat, my early morning coffee still warm in the cup holder. I'd been eating plums all morning and was now running late, so I didn't have time to pick up lunch. I found some peanuts in the passenger seat and washed those down with the coffee as I took a left onto Davis Avenue, both sides of which were lined with Jackson-owned fruit. The only other thing besides trees on this stretch of Davis was the massive Kingsburg Orchards compound; I took a right into the entrance and then continued down an unmarked road past a large Jackson-owned packing shed. Fruit that was too small, too gnarled, too blemished to pack was cascading down from the rear wall's cull chute. More fruit came out of that chute in thirty seconds than I would eat all year. Driving slowly along the narrow orchard road, I passed the occasional turnoff that gave me a glimpse down the rows of trees, extending as far as the eye could see. A third of a mile down the road, I came to another packing shed and then to the small, detached house that is the sales office for Kingsburg Orchards.

The receptionist told me that Mike would be a few minutes as he was just finishing a sales meeting. When I turned to sit down and wait, I saw Dale Janzen, the Industry Relations Director for the CTFA. I'd met him the previous March at the educational symposium in downtown Fresno. I reintroduced myself to Dale, who spent a good part of his week going around getting face time with growers, keeping track of what was going on, hearing people out, trying to get a sense of what was happening on the ground.

There was nothing else to talk about except the rotten market and the many variables that could be causing it. As we were going through them, the sales meeting let out and a stream of men filed down the hall toward us and went out the front door. Mike stopped in the door, looked back and forth between us, smiled, and said, "Who's first?"

Mike shook hands with Dale and then introduced himself to me.

"We were just talking about what's going on," Dale said, shaking his head. "Everybody thought it was a made-to-order year, but it's been real tough."

"Yeah, I've heard from guys I haven't talked to in twenty-five years asking me what I think we need to do about the market," Mike said.

"From what I can gather, the spot market's really, really bad right now. The program sales guys seem to be doing okay, but I can count them on one hand."

"Yeah, and they're lying," Mike said, smiling. He was one of those program sales guys.

I had only an hour or so with Mike, so after he and Dale quickly handled their business, I followed him back to a modern conference room where we sat down at a large table. A lot of packing shed/sales companies have a kind of "industrial parts supplier" vibe. Unmodernized, cubicle-ish, burnt coffee, brown ties. Kingsburg Orchards, though, felt more like an architect's office—not sleek exactly, but by agriculture sales office standards, pretty high-end.

Mike was philosophical about the market problems the industry was facing. Whatever other hard-to-define ills were afflicting California stone fruit in the long term, the short-term rise in costs was clearly hurting growers from all ends. "You've got to keep gas in your car and it costs a fortune to fill up at the pump. It makes me sick to fill up the tank. Plus, you've got to pay your mortgage, your power. Fifty percent of Americans, if not more, are getting squeezed financially. If you're squeezed financially, you go to the store and you buy the basics. What you eat is where you can pick and choose to save some money."

Like his uncle David, Mike was adamant about the importance of flavor, especially given the economic situation. In good years, when everything was selling, it was easy to get complacent and not look as hard at what was working and what wasn't. But a tough season like this one, he said, helped bring clarity to the industry. When the buyers were choosy, growers could plainly see where they could stand to make some improvements. And if the days of growing stone fruit that tasted like cardboard were waning, there was still, Mike said, a lot of room for improvement. There were still a lot of peaches, plums, and nectarines out there that tasted just okay, that didn't lead to what he called a " 'wow' eating experience."

"If somebody's going to pay two ninety-nine a pound or more for something, you can't have them saying, 'Oh, pthhtt!' and throwing the fruit away," he said. Stone fruit was competing with everything else in the store for the consumer's food dollars. As the market research had shown, stone fruit growers needed to attract repeat sales, to increase demand so that retailers would buy more fruit. The only way to do that, Mike said, was to grow and sell fruit that would render the person eating it near-speechless. " 'Oh! Oh! That's the best thing I've ever had!' That's what we want to hear. And to get it, you have to chase flavor."

Not only did you have to chase flavor, you had to market it well, too. Like Family Tree and its Flavor Safari line, Kingsburg Orchards had set up a couple of its own high-Brix, high-flavor lines. The most established was the Dinosaur Egg brand, which they had expanded over the years from just a single variety in late July and early August to a whole line of mottled fruit that ran from mid-May into October. In fact, the Dapple Dandy pluot, which was the original Dinosaur Egg, was now being phased out of the line completely in favor of larger, sweeter varieties that matured around the same time and that were controlled exclusively by the Jacksons.

The exclusivity made all the difference. Just look at what had happened to Dapple Dandy. While it was still in its infancy and there wasn't much of it out there, Dapple Dandy made the Jacksons a lot of money. As it took off, more and more growers wanted it, and since the people at the Dave Wilson Nursery made their money by selling trees, the more trees they sold, the better they did. But for a fruit grower, the number of trees out there mattered. A scarce variety fetched a higher price from buyers. If there was a glut of that variety and it was all coming off the tree at the same time, then buyers could more easily work the box price down. Plus, Mike said, when a lot of people planted a variety, you got a wide range of quality, diminishing the brand.

"With Dapple Dandy, people want to be first to market to

get a higher price. So they want to pick ten days early. The problem with Dapple Dandy is that it's fair at best unless you're patient with it and you wait to pick it at full maturity. But a lot of people start picking them too early and so the power of the variety gets diluted. So as we go after new varieties, the more control we can have—over the volume, over the standard it's picked at—the better."

That is why exclusives were important, and after slowly building out the Dinosaur Egg line, the Jacksons were intrigued when Glen Bradford approached them with his entire inventory of black-skinned, red-fleshed plums. The Jacksons had combined those plums with some similar Zaiger varieties and branded the line with the name Sugar Tree. "We're in complete control of them," Mike said. "I don't have to worry about somebody picking in front of me, because I'm the only one with those varieties. And if it's not sweet, then we won't put that sticker on it. That's eighteen to twenty-two Brix sugar, so the experience is always good. What you'll see this year, as the price gets cheaper, is that some guys try to put more in the box. Well, you cannot put more! You've got to put less! You've got to bring your standards higher and higher and higher, because there's so much else to choose from. There's cheap fruit everywhere out there—cheap melons, cheap grapes, cheap everything. To compete with that, you have to put your best foot forward. It's the same with guys who are shipping pluots. The guys who pick their Dapple Dandies green send their first load out and then they wait and wait and wait, wondering when the next call's coming. Well, it's not going to come unless you put good stuff forward. I think we're in a paradigm shift all across the industry. People are realizing that everything's got to eat well."

Mike had been looking at his watch for a while now, eager to get moving. I reminded him that I was hoping to see Wayne Adams's Dapple Dandies. He slapped the table and hopped up. If we got going, he said, we could also skip around the orchard and sample a few of the exclusive red-fleshed varieties that were going into the Sugar Tree line.

In his truck, we headed back toward the main road. We took a quick right onto one of the dirt turnoffs and headed into the thick of the orchard. He drove for a while and then coasted over to the left side of the road and leaned his head out the window to look at the trees. "Nope, too far," he said to himself, then reversed the truck for five seconds and stopped next to a row of trees that looked to me exactly like the row of trees we'd stopped in front of just moments before. "Here we go," Mike said, climbing out of the truck and tramping down the overgrown space between the rows.

"It's kind of a mess in here, because we're not really using this right now." He stopped in front of a harried-looking tree and gestured down the row. Here they were, the oldest Dapple Dandies in the Valley. He pulled a branch down so that he could reach a piece of fruit off the top of the tree. He tossed it to me. "A lot of guys are picking this right now, but it's too early." I bit into it. Sweet. A little crunchy. Mike was looking at a piece of fruit lower on the tree and close to the trunk. "See, it's not just when you pick the fruit. There are a lot of growing practices you can use to influence flavor. Sunlight makes sugar, so all the fruit at the top of the tree will get sweet. But to get fruit sweeter in the middle and bottom of the tree, you have to do things to get light in there. You have to capture the maximum amount of light." When I asked him about the newer varieties with which he planned to replace Dapple Dandy, he looked around and started walking back toward the dirt road. I dropped the fruit and followed. We crossed the road and walked over downed limbs and ducked under long ones drooping with fruit. Mike stopped and reached into a tree. The fruit looked like a bigger, darker Dapple Dandy. "We've got an exclusive on this one," he said as he handed it to me. It popped juicy and exposed a sweet and complex pinkish flesh. I kept eating it as we walked toward a half-acre test block the Jacksons had planted in 2002. They had planned to pull the test block out but then ended up leaving it in because it was near the sales office and they could get guests over to it easily for a quick sample (I'm happy to report). It had started them thinking about a project they were working on now. In one central plot, they were going to graft in one tree of every variety that made up the Dinosaur Egg and Sugar Tree lines. They were putting the plot right next to the sales office, so that they'd have all their premium stuff in one spot. It wouldn't be ready for a couple of years, but when it was finished they would block it off and call it the Garden of Eden.

Mike started walking really fast through the test block. His voice quickened. At least, his voice seemed to quicken. It could have just sounded that way to my own unstable senses. Mike stopped at a tree. He pulled down a dark plum. It was dark purple, almost black. He brushed off the bloom with his sleeve. "Here, try this." I took it and ate. The flesh was the reddest red

I've seen. It was the red of Snow White's lips, which was the red of her mother's blood. (Carried away here.) It was fairy tale–red fruit. It was a fairy-tale plum. "Don't eat the whole thing," Mike said. It sounded like a fairy-tale caution. I was about to say that out loud, but he was, fortunately, already off and up ahead. Who says that anyway?

"Okay," he shouted back at me, "come here. You've got to try this one." A black one with sugar spots. Brushed it off with his sleeve. Handed it to me. Watched as I took a bite. A tractor rumbled in the distance. "Man," I said by way of appreciation. "Yeah," he said, and then he was off "Okay, wait. Over here." I had a half-eaten plum in each hand. "Be careful," he said over his shoulder, laughing.

Eating plums out in the orchards of California, it was always easy for me to forget that the fruit was someone's business, that growers' livelihoods depended on it. The summer of 2007 would turn out to be a brutal season for many of them, comparable in its ugliness to 2004. The spot market was especially weak through August, when many growers harvested most of their fruit. By late summer, there were rumors that several large growers were planning to either consolidate or get out of agriculture altogether. The patriarch of one stone fruit mainstay was looking into development rights for his three-hundred-acre ranch, and another was so disgusted with the way the season had gone that he pulled more than five hundred acres of stone fruit and vowed never to grow another peach, plum, or nectarine in his life.

Rod Milton "ended up with black ink, but it wasn't pretty."

He'd picked a lot less fruit in 2007 than he had in 2006. Looking ahead, he was pessimistic. The plum volume was as low as it had been in years, and still the supply seemed to be way too high. In August, he'd stopped at the Wal-Mart in Sanger to check things out. "Plums were at sixty-nine cents a pound. And it was real good fruit. A little small, but *good* fruit. And it was great pricing for the fruit. So I sat there and watched, and I saw this guy walk right past the plums and fill up a bag with Washington Red Delicious apples at a dollar sixty-nine a pound. Red Delicious apples! I'd sit there and eat my foot before I'd eat a Red Delicious apple! You can do everything right in the field but it'll drive you crazy to see somebody pass by your fruit for something a dollar more per pound. I should have just stayed in the car and not ruined my week." When the dust cleared on the season, Rod considered pulling both his Flavor Kings and his forty-year-old Friars, but he left both alone. After the next summer, though, which was in many ways even worse than 2007, he finally decided to get rid of the Friars. Instead of putting in new plums, he kept that land empty. With the stone fruit market so bleak, he couldn't justify putting anything new in. The Flavor Kings? They're still there. He still has some hope for those.

The guys with program sales fared a little better through the end of the summer. They had lined up buyers for enough fruit to offset the lower demand from retailers. Both Jackson outposts—Family Tree Farms and Kingsburg Orchards—were focused on program sales, so they reported better-than-average years. David Jackson finished building his "top secret R&D facility" and was looking forward to populating it with the fruits he'd collected during his international walkabout, some of which were coming out of federal quarantine in the fall. With Family Tree leading the push, "plumcot" would eventually get the same color-based PLU codes that "plum" had. That would allow them to abandon the unwieldy word "pluot" and focus on marketing plumcots instead.

That was good news, too, for Kingsburg Orchards and its Sugar Tree line of Bradford-bred hybrid plums, a pile of which I was collecting in the makeshift basket I'd formed by turning up the front of my T-shirt. I trailed behind Mike as we made our way back to the truck in the sun.

The next morning, I was leaving California, flying out early from Oakland. After leaving Kingsburg Orchards, I would stop off at my hotel and pick up the boxes of fruit I had collected from the Zaigers, Bradfords, Miltons, and Jacksons. Driving north on 99, I would pass by the exits for Parlier and Reedley, Fresno and Merced, and the monster housing developments in between. For a while, as night fell, I would run alongside a freight train strung with empty cars through which I could make out the occasional lights of the Valley's western side. I would pass the hidden exit in Le Grand, where Glen Bradford and I had sat waiting for Mike Watts and his wife. Just outside of downtown Modesto, I would cut west and pass a motorcycle dealership, a barbershop, a bodega, a Mexican restaurant, an ice cream wholesaler. I would pass through blocks of modest homes and then a modest canal off the Tuolumne River. I would pass the school, the church, the Gallos, and the unassuming left turn at Grimes Avenue (and Bob's Taxidermy, too). Half an hour later, I would get on the interstate at the northwestern tip of the San Joaquin and make my way west toward Oakland. I would fall asleep at the wheel a couple of times and finally pull over to take a short nap. I would make it to a motel next to the airport and sleep unsoundly for a few hours, then awake to consolidate my stuff. A quick inventory would show that I had at least two hundred pieces of fruit and as much as I wanted to, I couldn't take it all. I'd eat a few pieces for breakfast, then empty all of it onto the bed and pick out the firmest pieces of the varieties I knew for sure I wanted to take with me—the Flavor Kings, the Grand Rosas, some O'Henry peaches. I would put those pieces on the bottom of one box. Then, I would stack several layers of fruit on top of that layer and fill the gaps with smaller varieties, like some Jerusalem apricots Rod Milton had given me. I'd fill the second box with as much fruit as I could fit into it. That would leave a grocery sack full, which I would give to the guy at the front desk of the motel. Only when I returned the rental car would I realize how much I still had; there was no way I could lug my duffel bag, computer bag, camera bag, and two boxes of very fragile fruit for the trip home. I would take the second box of fruit to the woman doing returns. She would look at me suspiciously and then open the box and gasp. "I love plums," she would say, "but I never buy them at the store!" (That may be hard to believe, but it's true.) With the remaining box of fruit in the overhead compartment, I would fly a circuitous route from Oakland to Islip, on Long Island, and then catch a dead-of-night train into Brooklyn. From the Bergen Street subway stop, I would walk the eight blocks or so to our friend Kristin's apartment, put down my box of fruit, crawl into the bed next to Elizabeth (who was eight months pregnant), and, thirty-odd hours after leaving the Valley, go to sleep.

But that was all still a long way off. In the orchard, Mike had found a few more of the Sugar Tree varieties. My fingers were flecked with blue fuzz from having wiped the juice onto the legs of my jeans. My stomach growled, and I could feel the heat in my cheeks. We were headed back to the sales office when Mike remembered one more plum that he wanted me to try. It was a black-skinned variety called Midnight Jewel, and it would go into the Sugar Tree line. "You shouldn't leave without trying it," he said, turning the truck around. We drove a couple of blocks, turned back around, and then stopped. Mike hopped out and looked down the row. "Nope." We drove a little farther without finding the right plot, and then we found ourselves at the end of the lane, in front of the sales office.

"Okay, well, I need to get moving," Mike said apologetically. "I mean, the thing is, you could eat fruit all day long."

I dawdled. "So Midnight Jewel? I'll keep an eye out for it."

"Yeah, and you know, the good thing is that there will probably be a few varieties next year that are even better than what you've had this year."

There was always going to be something new to try. I knew this to be true. Still, a part of me wanted to make one more pass to find Midnight Jewel, even if it meant, as it surely did, that it would only lead to another plum, which would lead to another and then another, and who knows where it would end?

ACKNOWLEDGMENTS

Thanks to Heather Dewar, Ann Finkbeiner, Sally McGrane, Andy Moody, and Val Wang for helping to get this thing started. Many other people at JHU contributed in ways big and small. In that cousinly way of his, David Kirkwood tried to get me to just say it. Brys Stephens was gracious when I needed pluots to come before Cookthink. Kristin Hohenadel has always set high standards. Sandy and Harrison Starr fed me, housed me, clothed me, and invited me to my first (and only) burial at sea. Leigh and Todd Richardson gave me a comfortable bed and good enchiladas. Elise, Alice, and Tom Bauer, pluot growers themselves, rejuvenated me with fettucine and red wine. Barbara Kafka gave me a great title. At Westfield Farm, Cella Langer, Amy Rick, Kim Wheeler, and Debby and Bob Stetson motivated me, and a good chunk of this book was written in the mornings before joining them to make cheese.

In researching this book, I've relied heavily on articles, papers, reports, and books by Paul Collins, Joan Didion, Peter Dreyer, John Gregory Dunne, Geoff Dyer, Bill Grimes (and everyone at the California Rare Fruit Growers), Victor Davis Hanson, U. P. Hedrick, Jules Janick, William Kahrl, Jim Krause,

Craig Ledbetter, John McPhee, David Mas Masumoto, James N. Moore, William Okie, Russ Parsons, David Ramming, Marc Reisner, Kevin Starr, and D. J. Waldie. Anyone who writes about Californian fruit must also acknowledge the work (and passion) of David Karp.

Scores of hospitable people in the San Joaquin Valley came to my aid, including Glen Bradford, Wayne Brandt, Carlos Crisosto, Dan Gerawan, Ray Gerawan, Gary Giese, Don Goforth, David Jackson, Mike Jackson, Dale Janzen, Herb Kaprielian, Bill Morris, Dovey Plain, Blair Richardson, Steve Strong, Corina Tamez, Russ Tavlan, Dean Thonesen, Robert Woolley, Betty and Floyd Zaiger, Gary Zaiger, and Grant Zaiger. I'm especially indebted to Leith Gardner and Rod Milton, both of whom showed incredible patience as I asked the same questions over and over and over. I hope none of these people regrets helping me.

I owe a ton to Molly Barton. It was to justify her early interest that I kept working on pluots. She also introduced me to PJ Mark at McCormick & Williams. From the moment he's been on the scene, this project has been blissfully free of drama. Tamara Staples took beautiful fruit and made it even more so. I'm grateful to Colin Dickerman for making space for the book at Bloomsbury and to Nick Trautwein for taking it on as his own and leaving it in much better shape than when he found it. Big thanks also to Amy King, Janet McDonald, Rachel Mannheimer, and Jenny Miyasaki for their contributions to the book.

For their encouragement and enthusiasm, thanks to all the Barrys, Hugheys, Smyths, Johnsons, Daths, and Campbells. My loving parents, Neila and Bill Brantley, have always encouraged my writing, even when I wasn't doing it. I wish Mildred and

Frank Cantey could read this; she taught me what to keep in and he taught me what to leave out.

When I'm with Elizabeth, I never want to be someplace else. (I don't know why I said this. It is true.) We discovered pluots and each other at roughly the same time, and when I told her I wanted to write a book about the fruit, she said, *I'd like to see you try.* I hope this pleases her as much as a good party.

A NOTE ON THE AUTHOR

Chip Brantley is the cofounder of Cookthink.com, a cooking and recipe Web site. A former food writer for the *San Francisco Examiner* and features writer for the *Albany Times Union,* he has contributed to *Slate,* the *Boston Globe,* the *Oxford American,* and *Gastronomica,* among others. Brantley was also the head cheese maker at Westfield Farm, an award-winning cheese company in Hubbardston, Massachusetts. A native of Alabama, he lives with his wife and son in western Massachusetts.